Let's HAVE A DOG Party!

20 Tail-Wagging Celebrations to Share with Your Best Friend

Ingrid E. Newkirk,
founder and president of
PeTA

Aadamsmedia
Avon, Massachusetts

Published by Adams Media, an F+W Publications Company
57 Littlefield Street
Avon, MA 02322
www.adamsmedia.com

ISBN-10: 1-59869-149-X
ISBN-13: 978-1-59869-149-8

Library of Congress Cataloging-in-Publication Data
Newkirk, Ingrid.
Let's have a dog party! / Ingrid E. Newkirk.
p. cm.
ISBN-13: 978-1-59869-149-8 (pbk.)
ISBN-10: 1-59869-149-X (pbk.)
1. Parties for dogs. I. Title.
SF427.45.N49 2007
636.7'0887—dc22   2007015787

Printed in Canada
J I H G F E D C B A

This publication is designed to provide accurate and authoritative information with regard to the subject matter covered. It is sold with the understanding that the publisher is not engaged in rendering legal, accounting, or other professional advice. If legal advice or other expert assistance is required, the services of a competent professional person should be sought.
—From a *Declaration of Principles* jointly adopted by a Committee of the American Bar Association and a Committee of Publishers and Associations

Many of the designations used by manufacturers and sellers to distinguish their product are claimed as trademarks. Where those designations appear in this book and Adams Media was aware of a trademark claim, the designations have been printed with initial capital letters.

Photo credits: All photography ©iStockphoto.com: page 10: Emilia Stasiak; page 21: Adam Waliczek; page 32: Jean Frooms; page 37: James Steidl; page 45: Fabio Frosio, Mark Yuill, and Sean Locke; page 55: Dmitry Koksharov; page 73: Eric Isselée; page 92: Christine Balderas and Byll Williams; page 142: Adam Waliczek; page 154: Libby Chapman; page 179: Jill Fromer; page 182: Michael Chen; page 185: Judi Ashlock; page 191: Gina Luck.

This book is available at quantity discounts for bulk purchases.
For information, please call 1-800-289-0963.

With apologies to the Beatles:

All you need is dog!
Dog is all you need!

———————————————

This book is dedicated to Sir, a dear dog who lived on a chain with no hope of a pat on the head or a kind word, let alone a party. Eventually, he was rescued. To find out how to help the Sirs in the world, turn to Chapter 14.

ACKNOWLEDGMENTS

My gratitude to the very kind man who came up with this idea in the first place; to Mary Ann Naples of The Creative Culture and Jennifer Kushnier at Adams Media for making it happen; to all the great people who sent me stories and photographs; to Jody Boyman, Tal Ronnen, Susan Ocean, and Laura Brown for permission to use their photographs; to Sara Chenoweth, who helped pull all the bits together; and to all the people who rescue dogs, give them homes, defend them from harm, and remember that they need to be loved and respected.

PREFACE

The Dogs Who Started It

Because far too often their humans are "too busy" to find time to walk them or play with them as often and for as long as they should, dogs get bored with their lives.

This book came about because of two wonderful dogs, a very energetic Jack Russell terrier named Nana and a withdrawn, scared little Westie named Mie Mie (Japanese for *little sister*). Mie Mie came from a breeder who kept her in a closet under the stairs and, as a consequence, is worried about everything.

Both dogs live together in the private staff hallway of a lovely hotel in Brighton, England. They belong to two very busy men who own the hotel. On the rare occasion when the men aren't working, they holiday overseas without the dogs and have hobbies, like flying, that do not include the dogs. So the dogs spend much of their time in the private hallway.

The hoteliers have always allowed me to walk the dogs when I visit, and I find my holiday days starting rather earlier than I would like because I can't stay in bed when I know these two are dying to go out. Like most dogs, they do not like to soil their area and so they "hold it" for as long as they can. We are barely out the door, in fact, when there is a pause for Nana and Mie Mie to take care of important business.

The hotel is less than a block away from a little grass square where they love to go, but the real attraction for them is the pebble beach and the boardwalk. Although these joys are just on the other side of their street, most days Nana and Mie Mie can only dream of and remember past expeditions, because they are locked in the hallway.

The first dog party I ever held was for them. After a great walk, I asked permission to take them up to my room. There they could look out at pedestrians on the promenade and bark at other dogs, smell the sea air when I opened the huge floor-to-ceiling bay windows just enough to accommodate two twitching muzzles, eat treats (we had peanut butter crackers and dog "chocolate" drops), and stretch out on the thick covers of my big bed.

And I discovered something important. Nana and Mie Mie couldn't have cared less about the party streamers and confetti I'd brought for the occasion. What they loved was a kind word— or actually, as many kind words as I could string together: *Good dog, good dog, good puppy. . .* ! They loved new sights and smells, and they loved companionship.

We played and played and had a barking good time.

They adored it!

CONTENTS

Let's Have a Dog Party!

FOREWORD
by Pamela Anderson

Kids and dogs need constant stimulation, and there's no short-age of that at my house. At the end of the day, the place looks like Saks after a sale. The only difference is that when playtime is over, the "kids" in the fur suits don't have to do any home-work. They nap while I pick up all the toys. Oh, for opposable thumbs (the dogs, not me; I already have a set).

Having dogs around as you learn about life definitely makes you well rounded and whole. It teaches understanding of those who may not speak the same exact language as you do, but who also have wants and needs—like a burning desire to chase muskrats at 2 A.M. or to bury those pink sweaters you make them wear when it gets chilly.

Dogs bring great joy and love. They hang on your every word—something it's hard to get a grown man to do unless you are giving him the football score. They are also eternally grate-ful for being rescued, so I try to rescue a bunch of them. In fact, I hang out at places like the Angel Pug Rescue, where I picked up a wonderful squashed-nose dog named Foo for my friend Natalie Raitano from *V.I.P.* All dogs deserve to be treated like V.I.P.s.

I love this book, especially the chapter about including kids in your dog party! My sons are growing up with dogs. The boys have been like brothers to my tiny Luca Pizzaroni Pasquini, and to my ancient-in-years but totally young-at-heart big fella, Star. Star's been my partner in crime forever. When I look at him, I can remember everything that's happened to the two of us in our years together in Hollywood.

There are so many great tips in *Let's Have a Dog Party!* to help you keep your dogs healthy and happy. There's even a section on water safety, which is important to my family, as we live at the beach. Some of our dogs are real surf hounds (that sounds like a breed, doesn't it?). Sometimes I feel like a *Baywatch* commercial, chasing the dogs into the surf to make sure they come out again in one piece. Especially Luca! She would keep right on swimming the Atlantic if she thought she had a chance of flirting with a royal corgi on the other side (getting fixed has not curbed her deeply romantic nature. I wonder who she gets that from?).

The tips here are totally me, because when you are a mom, you have to be on the lookout for all sorts of hazards, even ones that might drop out of the sky! I taught the kids to watch out that a hawk didn't get Luca, and I'm not kidding. I once rescued a Maltese who had been abducted by an owl and then somehow scrambled loose and survived!

The next time we go romping in the woods in Michigan, this book will be in my backpack. It reminds me to make sure the dogs stay hydrated, to ensure they wear proper ID in case they get spooked by Sasquatch or gunfire, and to carry plenty of towels so that my car doesn't look like a dirt-mobile when I load them up to go home to supper.

And, speaking of supper, I love the diet advice in *Let's Have a Dog Party!* It's practical and fun, with lots of ideas for yummy treats like doggie ice cream and special cookies (no sugar or onions for dogs, please). There are emotional treats, too, that mean the world to a dog, like kisses and hugs, patience, understanding, and words of praise. In fact, this whole book is such a treat that I hope you treat yourself and your dog to it!

Wait. Someone's howling. It's my handsome Star either complaining again that he can't open the refrigerator door with his psychic powers or reminding me that it's time to run outside and give the seagulls their workout. Gotta go!

INTRODUCTION
by Bill Maher

Let's Have a Dog Party! is the best argument I've heard for a three-party system in America—and my vote is definitely going to the dogs. If you have a dog, you need to buy this book, read it, and commit it to memory. Because unlike conservatives, dogs aren't interested in things like eliminating taxes on yachts and diamonds. Unlike liberals, they aren't waiting for Rush Limbaugh's next drug bust. In fact, dogs never worry about presidential primaries, affirmative action, violent video games, or who's going to win *American Idol—you* are their whole world. If they are only a tiny part of yours, something is very wrong.

This book will help you embark on a joyful twelve-step-like program to make your dog happy. ("Hi, my name is Bill, and I am a dog-aholic. I acknowledge that I am powerless over my love for my dog.") You won't believe how easy it is. The divorce rate would be zero if spouses were as easy to please as dogs. What does it take? A sandbox in the backyard, a bunch of sticks, some rotten seaweed to roll in, a hug. Ingrid Newkirk has a zillion good ideas on how to please your dog, so I guarantee you'll find the perfect party theme for your pooch.

As you will see, your party for your dog can be a fancy, dress-up do or a muck-around-in-the-mud affair. You can have lots of guests or just the two of you. My favorite is the luau, where the people arrive dressed in moo-moos and the dogs go nude, tear the piñata apart with their teeth, and chow down on Hawaiian poi, doggie-style (peanut butter stirred into cooked Cream of Wheat).

If that's not your bag, pull out the weird shorts with the suspenders, check the vinegar content of the sauerkraut, and invite your favorite dachshund to an Oktoberfest. Or how about a "celebrate your dog's sterilization" party? These ideas only *sound* wacky. In fact, they all hold an essential truth: It is crucial to see the world from your dog's point of view if you want to make him happy. True, the polka music is for my pleasure, but the hide-the-treat-in-my-back-pocket game is for the dog, who, as Homeland Security well knows, loves to use his sniff-and-search skills to find rewards.

Ingrid Newkirk's brilliant array of ideas is for those who already understand this, as well as for those who haven't yet realized that living in the same backyard and eating the same dry kibble day after day for a dozen years is like turning on the TV every night to find only reruns of *The Andy Griffith Show*. She reminds us, too, that we shouldn't congratulate ourselves on our elevated IQ. Show me a Rhodes scholar who can find a skier buried under an avalanche or detect cancer by sniffing someone's face and then we'll talk about human superiority.

In short, *Let's Have a Dog Party!* is the essential handbook for making your dog happy. If you, like me, would rather play in the park with your dog than stand around at a Hollywood shindig, this book is for you.

AUTHOR'S INTRODUCTION

England's Princess Anne went storming into court to defend the honor of her scrappy bull terrier, Dotty, who had taken a bite out of two children during a walk in Windsor Great Park. President Clinton seemed only able to take comfort in his dog, Buddy, during his most difficult days in the White House. And Martina Navratilova used to smuggle her dog, KD, aboard the Amtrak train rather than leave him at home (luckily, the statute of limitations has run out on that infraction!). As you know from every tabloid photograph, starlets would never want to be caught drinking cocktails onboard a yacht in Saint-Tropez or entering the latest nightclub without a tiny doggie as "arm candy."

But, all that aside, no one's dog is more precious than . . . yours!

Perhaps Bill Maher said it best when he introduced Sir Paul McCartney at a People for the Ethical Treatment of Animals (PETA) gala in Hollywood. "I love my dogs," he said. "They're the only people I know who, when I step through the door, greet me like I'm the Beatles!"

It's true, of course. Even if you can't sing a note, have no discernible talents, and look as if you've slept in a hedge, your dog adores you. That tail wags for you.

Dogs are always ready to show that love. Michael Tobias, one of the world's great souls and an author of many weighty tomes on humanity, the environment, and religion, told me a story about a time, many years ago, when he was conducting field studies in Yosemite National Park. Accompanying him was a wolf hybrid (part Samoan, Michael thinks) named K.

The two of them slept in a remote cave until one day, K vanished. For two days, Michael searched but to no avail. By the third day, Michael was petrified, panicking, imagining K coming to a bad end because it was now the high summer, the tourist season, and the park was full of RVs, ice cream trucks, and a couple of million visitors whom this long-legged creature would no doubt scare. He was sure to be shot, trapped, or run off.

K had never been to Yosemite. In fact, he had scarcely ever left his sanctuary high in the Rockies where he usually lived. Michael searched frantically throughout 100 square miles of territory but could not find him. Finally, Michael had to shift camp, moving away into the heart of the valley.

Later that week, in the middle of the night, K came out of the woods. He licked Michael's cheeks, and collapsed asleep on his sleeping bag. Somehow he had detected Michael's trail, followed his scent, found his campsite in an altogether new location, from amid easily 500,000 other humans in the immediate vicinity. He had found his way twenty-odd miles from the original cave to that sleeping bag, and, as Michael recounts, "had apparently done so with the ease of an albatross circling the planet on a whim." What love!

So, how do you reward your adoring fan(s) for such unflagging devotion? Some people buy their dogs jeweled collars, make sure they eat off nothing but the finest China, and treat them to limo rides around town. But dogs don't really care for frippery and flash. They aren't happier if their own wardrobes contain more sweaters and coats than J.Lo's. And they certainly don't want to spend much of their lives inhaling varnish at the beauty parlor. What a dog needs is a party!

A dog party can be very elaborate, very chic, very impressive, be the talk of the town and knock the socks off any human beings lucky enough to score an invitation, but it can also be as simple as simple can be, as easy as pie, and as plain as Jane. And, from a dog's perspective, that's just fine!

Whatever the theme or whatever effort goes into it, a dog party is definitely not only super fun, but also important for your dog and for you. It provides a great bonding experience that means the world to that special dog in your life. It is the quickest, sweetest, most appreciated way to show your love and affection. And love given is like the proverbial bread that is cast into the water that comes back hundredfold! You'll end up with enough dog kisses to skip washing your face for at least a week.

A dog party can also make up, in a trice, for some of your almost unpardonable shortcomings: those times, for example, when you have come home late, tired, or cross. Or (egads!) when you have rushed in, changed your clothes, and left again for the evening forgetting that your angel, your faithful companion, has been lonely and bored, sitting, legs tightly crossed for a distressing and unmentionable reason, staring at the wall for hours, waiting patiently, aching for your return, unable even to hum or whistle to pass the time.

That's where *Let's Have a Dog Party!* comes in. It delivers the most important present of all: *you* and your undivided attention to your dog—*exactly* what your dog loves most.

Everything in this book has been carefully field-tested. In cozy living rooms and in the much-loved Bea Arthur PETA Dog Park (which is populated by dogs and, as I discovered by accident, by quite a few people looking for a dog-friendly person to date) and in many other locales, the dog party has proven to be a great time for a great friend.

So now that you know how vital this event is to your canine companion, what's keeping you?

Forget doing the laundry tonight. Salvador Dali never did his laundry, and look how successful he was! (Actually, Salvador Dali rolled in goat dung before he went to bed, showing he could really relate to dogs and their aspirations.)

It's time for you to declare, "Let's Have a Dog Party!" Your dog will be so pleased, she'll blush like a Pharaoh hound (whose ears, nose, and eyes become pink when they are excited or happy).

The fun starts right now!

1

How to Say "I LOVE You"

(Or, Speaking Your Dog's Language)

"100 percent of respondents reported that they have said 'I love you' to their dog."

—Glamour *magazine poll*

Loving words are a key element in *Let's Have a Dog Party!,* by which I mean that a dog party can absolutely consist solely of you saying things to your dog, and nothing more. No cake, no nothing. Just give your dog your undivided attention and talk to her. I am going to give you a list of just the right words at the end of this chapter.

Here's one reason why this simple plan works:

In 2005, researchers at the Max Planck Institute for Evolutionary Anthropology in Leipzig revealed their findings after having studied a little dog named Rico. The researchers came to the conclusion that dogs can understand more than 200 spoken human words *without any specific instruction whatsoever!*

That's more words than I know in French despite *eight years* of special tuition. I have an excuse: English people are the most hopeless dolts when it comes to learning foreign languages. My theory is that the British Empire was started for the sole reason that *everyone else* in the world would be compelled to learn to speak Henry VII's language. That way, Henry and his successors—who ruled almost 500 million people at one point—ran no risk whatsoever of looking foolish for not knowing everyone *else's* tongue.

So, what *are* the words dogs understand?

Well, anyone who has decided to do something about the condition of a dog who has just rolled in horse manure or who has fallen down after trying to climb a tree after a squirrel knows that B-A-T-H and V-E-T have to be spelled out or our angels will disappear into the woodwork. In fact, in those cases, most adult dogs can do the spelling, too, and you have to write the words on a slip of paper and pass it along to anyone else who needs to get out the hose or know where you're off to.

Linda Miranda confirmed this when she adopted Toad, a greyhound found abandoned at a racetrack. In time, she says, Toad learned an impressive human vocabulary, and it became necessary to spell certain words or turn up the radio to hold a conversation about anything involving him.

In one of his famous stories, Rudyard Kipling has a dog tell the reader, "I know all about people's talking. No good say[ing] R.A.T.S. or W.A.L.K.S. to me. I know!" True enough.

"Want to go for a walk?" and "Dinnertime!" are shoo-ins too. Other words dogs quickly cotton on to relate to toys and food and other subjects that interest them mightily, given that most of their lives involve sitting and waiting for permission to have treats or go outside to smell the world. They also remember not only the smell but the names of people and other animals of their acquaintance.

Dog expert Jayn Meinhardt says, "We expect dogs to understand our language, yet we fancy ourselves the more intelligent ones and cannot understand theirs. We all need to be more attuned to these wondrous, intelligent beings and their needs as they have to try so hard to fit into our world and we have too often not given them the world that they deserve."

Then there are the words all dogs—from those who are carried underarm in padded bags to those whose whole lives consist of being so neglected that they are stuck outside on a heavy chain more suitable for hauling a tractor-trailer than anchoring a dog—ache to hear. The words that make a dog's ears stick up intently, eyes sparkle, and lips curl back in a big, fat grin (not to be mistaken for a growl).

Those special words include your dog's own name spoken with deep affection, and all imaginable words of love and praise, including your favorite special love names for your dog—like "angel cakes," my personal favorite—the terms of endearment that you would no doubt be embarrassed to hear over the office intercom.

Dog Tales

A dog walked into a Western Union office and took a form to fill out. He wrote: "Woof. Woof. Woof. Woof. Woof. Woof. Woof. Woof. Woof."

The clerk examined the form and politely said to the dog, "There are only nine words here. You could send another Woof for the same price."

"But," the dog replied, "that would make absolutely no sense at all!"

What Their People Say

I have come to think people should be hit with a rolled-up newspaper if they ever "woof" at a dog. Face it—you don't speak the language, you don't know what you're saying. And your intonation is appalling. It's worse than strangers trying to imitate my

English accent. When they do I'm tempted to hit them with a copy of the *Times* of London.

Ask people if they can understand their dogs and if their dogs can understand them, and you will be regaled with stories. Many dogs have even found ways to communicate effectively without saying a thing. For instance, Glenda, a mixed marvel who lives with the founder of the Animal Rights Foundation of Florida (ARFF), Nanci Alexander, will tilt her head at Nanci when she has had the unmitigated gall to do something Glenda doesn't appreciate; accountant Amber Wilt's dog, Dock, gets into bed and chews on Amber's hair to make her get up and get cracking; and Bill Killion, a Humane Society volunteer, reports, "My twelve-year-old basset, Clifford, who we rescued almost six years ago, uses a most interesting form of communication when he thinks it's time for me to go to work. In the morning, when I'm sound asleep, he grabs my wrist in his mouth and tugs at it until I wake up. When I finally am awake, he lies down again and goes straight back to sleep, his job done!"

TV commentator Andy Rooney once said that he hates to hear dogs barking. Not because he's a curmudgeon and not because, like so many other people, he finds the noise annoying, but because he is sensitive. He believes that the barking dog is trying to tell him something, and he can't help because he doesn't know what he's being told.

As for complexity, dog mother extraordinaire, Elaine Sloane, is amazed by the variety in her own dog's language.

"When I come in from being out for a while," she says, "Teddy Bear howls. He becomes amazingly vocal! He comes right up to me and whines, howls, and carries on, using many different intonations. It is like Chinese tonal language, and I can definitely tell he is advising me in no uncertain terms that it was wrong of me to leave him behind and that I must certainly not do it again." What a charming dog!

I've long suspected that dogs not only have language but that they have dialects too, just as French crows are known to caw in different "accents" depending on where in France they are born. Dogs can probably tell if you are from Birmingham, Alabama, or Birmingham, England, by listening to your inflections.

Of course, French *chiens parlent français très bien*, as evidenced by all those dogs in the cafés near the *Tour d'Eiffel* who understand *perfectly* when their mistresses enquire "*un petit morceau, chérie?*" as a glass dish of some delicacy appears in front of the chaise on which Pierre has "*asseyez-vous*-ed." Our prim health inspectors, having been born irrationally phobic, would have *une conniption!*

Recently, I came across a study that bears out my language theory. According to the Canine Behaviour Centre in the United Kingdom, dogs' voices differ in tone and pitch depending on where they live and how their guardians sound. The study concluded that Scottish dogs and those who live, as did the Beatles, in Liverpool have deeper barks and growls than dogs living in other parts of the British Isles. So there you have it!

"I Can't Hear You!"

Sometimes it pays to listen extra hard. One day, PETA case-worker Teresa Chagrin's dog Bingo, who was rescued from the Midwest floods, would not let Teresa leave for work. Although he weighs only about thirty pounds, he kept blocking her way out the door and then herded her onto the balcony. There she heard what Bingo was worried about. There were sounds of a dog barking in obvious distress. Teresa promised Bingo that she would check it out, squeezed out the door, and followed the barks. They led her to a dog who was tied to a fence by a rope that was so tangled that his front feet were barely touching the ground.

Says Teresa, "I was able to help that dog only thanks to Bingo. Bingo had been rescued himself and knew to rescue that dog. Now I listen really closely to Bingo, because he is a genius with a really big heart."

Not that all dogs are anxious to communicate on every occasion. Simone Reyes, who is hip-hop mogul Russell Simmons's right-hand woman, has a story or two to tell about her pit bull mix Stevie, named after Stevie Nicks.

Simone found Stevie when she was on her way to the Astro-land amusement park in Coney Island, a place that is known for packs of homeless dogs. Stevie was born stone deaf and Simone learned that she had been "living rough" on Surf Avenue for quite a while. Neighbors said that people on the block would give her scraps of pizza. Stevie would enjoy some but then carefully bury the rest under a tree so that she could ration it out for herself to eat later.

"Always thinking ahead, my Stevie," says Simone.

It makes Simone laugh now to think that while some dogs pretend not to hear their person call to them, being deaf, Stevie has to go to extra lengths to ignore Simone when she wants her to come inside or do something else Stevie doesn't want to do. Simone says, "When that happens, Stevie simply pretends not to *see* me. If she is off on her own, running in a field, really enjoying herself and I am 'calling' her to come back from a long distance—you can usually spot me looking as if I am doing jumping jacks to get her to see me—I see her sneak a peek at me and then quickly avert her eyes. She is clearly thinking to herself, 'If she doesn't know I see her, I can get away with this!' Every day with her is funny, and every day is a blessing."

It's up to You

So how do you tell your "blessing" that you care? No matter how sophisticated your dog is, he wants to hear those special words that translate into "I love you" as sure as even Kung Fu masters enjoy a good cuddle. These words are the very ingredients—and all the ingredients you will need—to throw a great dog party! Let me give you some tips and a script.

First, if you naturally sound like bass-voiced Bea Arthur, you will want to keep the party mood upbeat by purposely pitching your voice a little higher than usual. A low voice can be intimidating and may be interpreted, dog forbid, as a growl. A soprano voice is not generally threatening to dogs; perhaps it makes them think of puppies, mice, and kittens and gets them all mushy inside.

Second, brace yourself. Baby talk is encouraged and anyone who doesn't like it should move out of earshot.

All you have to do to get the ball rolling is to simply sit down on the floor (so your dog doesn't have to look up at you for once and suffer compressed discs in her neck) and read the "Words Dogs Love to Hear," page 20, out loud to your canine companion.

How you read it is the most important thing.

Live it up! Feel the words!

Do what great narrators do and make each word come alive with emotion. Imagine you are trying out for the lead in *101 Dalmatians* or *Love Story.*

Read from your heart, with feeling and love.

Enjoy each moment. Relish the time together. Don't skip, don't rush. Don't feel foolish, don't blush!

Think of it this way: Your dog does silly things that amuse you. Now it's your turn. One of my favorite examples of the not only touching but plain daft ways that dogs cheer people up is from Karen Porreca, PETA's librarian and an amateur dog behaviorist.

Karen was mourning the death of Druzhok, a dog who was noticeable most of all for his big, wide smile. Druzhok smiled at everyone! He had lived a long and healthy life, and one morning, after Druzhok's death, Karen was feeling pretty miserable thinking about him when another of her dogs, Rogan, ran and found a rubber ball. Instead of asking to play, he seemed to deliberately set about to chew the ball in half. Then he held it in his mouth with the "cup" part up so that his lips hung over it, making him seem as if he were smiling. He ran up to Karen and stuck his "smiling" face in her face, all excited and snorting, as if to say, "Look, Mom! *I'll* smile for you!"

Your dog will swell with pride when he hears you directing a whole stream of positive words at him. I guarantee he will look and feel special, complimented, flattered, proud, and as happy as Angelina Jolie at an adoption agency.

The message your dog will get from your recital is, "My person is focusing on me. My person loves me, really loves me! Yippee!"

Your words will comfort and soothe your dog and ensure that the memory of the party, whether it was a week ago or yesterday (which we hope it is, every day), will fill your dog's heart during those lonely times when you are otherwise engaged. (Must I mention that this should not encourage you to ever be otherwise engaged?)

So, warm your vocal cords as Pavarotti does before launching into *Nessun dorma* and you'll be ready to woof it up! Ready? Here you go.

Words Dogs Love to Hear

To be read aloud, with great feeling and enthusiasm!

Good! Good! Good! Good!
Good puppy! Good puppy! Good puppy! What a sweetie!
Good! Good! Good! Good!
We love you! Good puppy! Good puppy! Good puppy!
You're so special! Extra, extra special!
Good! Good! Good! Goodie, lovey dovey puppy!
Lovey dovey good, good puppy!
Who's a good puppy? What a good puppy! Good puppy!
     Good puppy!
Good! Good! Good puppy! We love you!
Good! Good! We love you! Good puppy! Good puppy!
Good! Good! Good! Good!
Who's so good? Who's such a silly puppy? Good, good!
     Good, good!
Good puppy! Good puppy! Good puppy! Good puppy!
We love you! We love you!
Yes we do! Yes we do!

There, you did it! Who's wagging her tail? Who? Yes you are.
Oh, yes you are!

2

Plain and Simple or a FANCY PANTS Party?

"When Richard Sheridan produced the hit play *The Caravan* at the new Drury Lane Theatre in London at the turn of the nineteenth century, it featured a dog, named Carlo, who every night onstage jumped into a pool to rescue a child. One night the principal actor ran up to say something terrible had happened.

'What is it?' asked Sheridan.

'I've lost my voice,' said the actor. 'Can't you tell?'

'Oh, is that all?' Sheridan replied. 'I thought something had happened to the dog!'"

—*Robert Henderickson,*
The Book of Literary Anecdotes

There are lots of suggestions in this book for exciting ways to fancy up your dog party, but never lose sight of one fact: All that is important is how the dog is doing. We add frills and frippery and otherwise fancy things for ourselves and for our human friends' amusement. As for the dogs, they care about something quite different. Jerome K. Jerome got it right when he said of the dog, "He never makes it his business to inquire whether you are in the right or wrong, never asks whether you are rich or poor, silly or wise, sinner or saint. You are his pal. That is enough for him."

So the principle behind the party is what counts and, quite frankly, *all* that counts. King Louis XIV may have thrown "divine" parties at the Palace of Versailles that boggled the mind in their quest to impress, with live chess pieces and fountains running with wine, but your dog doesn't care. What he cares about is the fact that you are going to show him that you are fond enough of him to pour all your love and affection into this special event just for him. Your undivided attention is the greatest gift. The other big gifts are respect, freedom, and praise. And the occasional toy.

When it comes to not being bowled over by fancy stuff, I can definitely relate. When I was a little girl of about six or so, my parents proudly presented me with a Victorian dollhouse that was very fancy indeed. It had, I am told by my mother, exquisitely furnished rooms. The detail was marvelous, with landscapes and portraits on the walls, clocks and ornaments on the mantelpieces over the fireplaces, even little fireplace tools like a grate, bellows, and a brush for the cinders. There were real lace tablecloths, tiny potted aspidistra, cut-glass chandeliers, children's books on the tiny shelves, and handcrafted dolls representing the well-dressed parents and their children—the girls wearing smocks and one carrying a hoop. There was even a miniature terrier dog.

The very first week I was given this special, expensive dollhouse, I went to visit my friend down the street and fell in love with *her* dollhouse! We swapped.

You can just imagine the looks on my parents' faces when I came home, flushed with pride, to show them my new dollhouse—a total piece of rubbish banged together with pieces from an old orange crate!

Dogs are pretty much of the same disposition. Take Bonita, for instance: She is a tiny and very feisty brown mixed Chihuahua whom PETA staffer Teresa Gibbs brought back from her grueling work improving rundown animal shelters in Puerto Rico. Teresa plucked Bonita from behind the bars of a filthy dog pound where numerous animals had died of disease. The next thing Bonita knew, she was under a cabin seat, flying to Washington.

I had the pleasure of having Bonita's company for a few months, working out her kinks you might say, until the perfect home came along. Bonita had lived on the street, it's true, and had gone without even the basics for a long time, but unlike most humans who go up in the world and are thereafter partial to the "finer things" in life, Bonita was no parvenu. She was true to her roots.

I offered her a comfy, fluffy-pillowed bed under my desk, but she immediately seized ownership of a barren shelf within a cabinet by the wall and moved inside it, nudging the door open with her nose and dragging her blanket behind her. Peeking out from her odd observation platform, she took to leaping out like a jack-in-the-box to ambush every unsuspecting visitor to my office.

Her favorite pleasures were the same as almost every dog's: very simple. During her convalescence from her ordeal, for example, which had left her with a rotten coat and a voracious appetite (giving a new meaning to the phrase "gutter mouth"), Bonita spent a weekend in Atlantic City, New Jersey. There, as she bounded along the sands, she demonstrated an uncanny ability to detect a chicken bone buried deep underground with more accuracy than professional beachcombers with their high-priced metal detectors could find whole sets of bedsprings just a couple of inches below. I spent far more time removing the bones from her firmly clenched teeth, under strenuous protest, than I spent putting sun block on my nose, which was a lot.

Bonita eventually did all right for herself. She now lives in absolute luxury in Malibu with a wonderfully animal-sympathetic couple, cartoonist Berkeley Breathed and his wife Jody Boyman, and their virtual "pack" of rescued dogs. And, although everything about her life has changed, including her name (Bonita is now "Pilar"), her tastes remain positively plebian.

Knowing this, when I find myself on a beach, I think back to her Atlantic City weekend and force myself to pick up smelly things that the tide has washed up. I pop them into an envelope and mail them to her. Jody has told me that she holds her nose, opens the package of rotting seaweed and decomposing crab limbs and fish spines, lets Pilar roll in the ordure (what I call her "sushi roll"), and then gives her a B-A-T-H.

Now, there's an idea for a party theme!

Catering to Your Dog's Desires and Dreams

Exactly who is your dog? What goes on in that sacred chamber between those floppy or perky ears? What secret longing and unfulfilled fun can you unleash? Is your dog like U.S. Olympic luge team six-time World Cup medalist Christian Niccum? Christian was going about his life in Minnesota when, one day, just because a luge team came to town, he discovered that—who knew?—he wanted to ride the ice bullet more than anything else he'd ever done. And he wanted to ride it over and over and over and over and over again. In other words, has your dog's dream not yet arrived?

Dogs have many talents, often hidden, some quite useful. Sometimes when he was writing a poem, Wordsworth would walk along, reciting the lines to his dog. He felt that if he picked the wrong word, a cacophonous word, or if the rhyme was wrong, his dog's hackles would rise and his "dog-critic" would show disapproval by barking.

So ponder this: Is there some unfulfilled talent, wish, or pleasure that it is your duty, as the controller of your dog's almost criminally restricted life, to ferret out of her? It doesn't have to be about becoming the best, but it could bring both of you insight and joy.

I discovered quite by accident that my dog, Ms. Bea, went nuts over curry and samosas—in fact, any really spicy food I picked up from the local Indian carryout. And it's guaranteed that your dog also has all sorts of secret cravings and talents that you can find if you set aside the time to try to figure it out.

> "When I was a kid, our dog loved snorting up dandelion spores, just loved it, which is how she got her name."
>
> —California "dog person" Christy Griffin, talking about her parents' dog, Dandelion

Since learning of Ms. Bea's ecstasy over chili sauce, I have conducted taste tests for animals entering my care and learned a lot (see Chapter 10), but there's much more than a dog's palate to consider. Dogs are quirky folk, and if you don't explore their crevices, you may go to your grave unaware that your dog longed, for example, to take a shower.

Once she'd discovered the shower, Teenie, a mixed Newfoundland, started banging on the shower door with such force that Tom Rayland, the construction engineer who had found Teenie in the California desert, decided he had no choice but to replace the glass for safety's sake and, when he can't lure Teenie into the yard before he turns on the shower, he's gotten used to having a nearly 100-pound dog sharing the shower stall with him.

Teenie isn't alone. A dog called Tazzie jumps straight into the bathtub if anyone leaves the door even slightly ajar, and then jumps back out again to go fetch her plastic frog and other favorite things. Her person says that she loves putting her head entirely under water in the bathtub to play with her toys.

Singer Mariah Carey revealed that she bathes with her dog. She says, "If I'm running a bath, all of a sudden I'll hear a splash and Jack will have jumped into the tub. I'm like, 'It's Jack in the tub again, swimming around.' Jack loves the jets on pools and hot tubs, and dives down to bite at the water coming out of them." Mariah has included Jack—or Jackson P. Mutley—in so many of her music videos, he now has a string of fan clubs.

Dog experts Jayn and Tom Meinhardt's discovery was easier (and drier) to live with. They had adopted Snickers from a shelter three years before they discovered an interesting aspect of her earlier life.

It happened when Jayn was thinking about something, got the answer, and snapped her fingers. Suddenly Snickers sat down and looked up at Jayn expectantly. It took a minute for the penny to drop. "Aha," thought Jayn. "Finger clicking is often used in dog obedience classes to let a dog know that a new command is about to be given."

Jayn started giving Snickers commands. "Sit," "Stay," "Come," and "Heel." And Snickers immediately did everything exactly right, even though she had not heard those words in at least three years! She would even "roll over" on command, although, with her newfound fat little tummy, it took some effort.

Jayn was so happy to have found a piece of the Snickers puzzle, although she realized that if Snickers remembered the words, the poor dog must surely also remember the person who had taught them to her and subsequently dumped her.

Things Your Dog Might Like

- Showers
- Winking
- Other animal species
- A dog (or cat) companion
- New foods (except those listed on page 167!)
- Musical toys
- Puzzles

Here's another idea. If you've never bought your angel a musical or talking toy, give it a whirl. Some dogs *don't* like them so you can stop there, but other dogs go bananas over them. Not just the squeaky toys, but the ones that play a tune or "speak."

My mother dog-sits for a little Shih Tzu named Boogie, and his absolute favorite toy in the whole world is a ridiculous lumberjack doll called "The Perfect Husband." This doll says things like, "No hurry, darling. Take your time getting ready. I could wait for you all day." Boogie has a host of toys to choose from but takes most delight in hitting the lumberjack in the stomach with his paw, over and over again, to make him come up with yet another phrase a woman is unlikely to hear in real life, such as, "Honey, that ball game means nothing to me. I'd rather go shopping with you any day."

One of airline pilot Dick Rybak and his wife Sheila's beautiful dogs was so fond of her musical toy that she could not bear to put it away at the end of the day. Sheila says she has woken up many a night to the sound of "We Wish You a Merry Christmas." No matter how annoying it is to miss out on a good night's sleep, Sheila can never stop laughing when she hears that tune.

Perhaps so would humane educator Patricia Trostle's dog, Bailey, who likes to play Trading Post. The game is dependent upon more than one person having something to swap. Bailey particularly likes to trade her snack for someone else's. If you give her a cookie or biscuit and then go and sit down with a snack or food of your own, she'll bring you her cookie and actually toss it at you—sometimes right up on your lap—so she can have yours instead.

Now here's an odd question: Have you *winked* at your dog lately? If not, you may be missing out. Karen Porreca, an amateur dog behaviorist, swears that almost every dog can learn how to wink back at you really easily. She says you just have to catch their gaze and then give them a deliberate, slightly exaggerated wink while at the same time saying, "Wink?" in a chirpy voice.

"It only takes a few repetitions before they wink back at you. It's amazing. You can practically see them thinking about it. And sometimes they'll experiment by blinking first. The only thing is that you don't want to give them performance anxiety, so if they appear uncomfortable (by looking away), then you should stop and maybe try again later but not pressure them, because, like most things, they take it seriously."

Perhaps Karen winked when she told me this!

And then there are interspecies friendships that shouldn't be missed. Some dogs fall in love with cats, particularly young kittens, others with lizards, rats, and birds. As long as the introductions are carried out with respect and precautions are taken, such mingling can be a bit like the Café at the End of the Universe in the *Hitchhiker's Guide to the Galaxy*, all different sorts hanging out together amicably.

The Frisks's dog, Lucky, a pit bull who had been abandoned as a puppy, is interested in birds but not in the way you might think. He likes to play with the crows in the family's yard and crows love the sport; they are notorious for teasing dogs and other animals. They will even feign sleep to get an animal to come over to them so they can play a trick. The crows on the Frisks's property—a former avocado orchard outside San Diego—sit atop of the tall avocado trees and caw at Lucky until he charges at the tree. At the moment Lucky comes up to the trunk, they fly off to the next tree to do the same thing all over again. This goes on and on. They are cawing and Lucky is racing and barking, probably thinking he is going to take off in the air and actually catch them. Everyone has a grand old time.

You may also learn things that you didn't know your dog *doesn't* like when you experiment with this and that, and then you can do your best to make sure that such objectionable substances, objects, or beings are given a very wide berth.

Researcher (not animal researcher!) Matthew Mongiello's dog, Hunter, hated two things in life with a passion: squirrels and the ceiling fan. For some reason, he associated them both with the same word. So if you said "squirrel," Hunter would first rush to the window, but once there, seeing nothing, he would redirect his wrath to the fan, spinning in circles, barking, and bouncing off all the furniture trying to reach it. It was a word the Mongiellos learned not to use in their house because all hell would break loose for about ten minutes.

What dogs don't like is sometimes a mystery. Young Christopher McDonough's parents' dog, Alexander the Grape, hated watermelons. Not the *taste* of them—he never got that intimate with one—but the mere *sight* of them.

During the summer the McDonough family always had a watermelon or two from their grandmother's garden sitting in a basket on the floor. As soon as Alex saw one, he would bark at it—even when it was just sitting there. Later, he started to notice that other things resembled watermelons—balloons, basketballs, footballs—and started warning them that, if they didn't shape up, he was going to get them too. One day, when everyone was out, a watermelon must have become particularly offensive, and he attacked. The family came home to find him covered in red watermelon stickiness and the house a wreck. Alexander had finally put a watermelon in its place, and he never bothered with them again!

So, in a busy world, it's worth setting time aside to stop and explore your dog's psyche. Give some thought to his peculiarities and figure out what he might miss and what you might help him rid the house of—like watermelons, perhaps?

3

A Few Words About Dog Party ETIQUETTE

"If she's out with me and sees someone close by in a hat, she'll try to take it off them. If I wear a scrunchie in my hair, she'll take that out too."

—*Patricia Trostle, a humane educator, talking about her dog, Bailey*

Do be sure that all human guests know in advance how they are expected to behave at a "doggie do." Give them a heads-up as to what's going to go on, how to dress, what to bring, and so on so that there are no rude surprises for them or you.

Make sure your guests realize that, at a dog party, jumping, digging, and occasional slobbering are not only allowed, they are *de rigueur.* You might advise anyone who is going to attend the affair to dress accordingly, perhaps in overalls. You can always call it a country hoedown theme. Or have your guests dress in coveralls and call it a car mechanics' ball. The latter might see a positive RSVP from Tom and Ray Magliozzi, the extremely dog-friendly "Click and Clack" from National Public Radio's *Car Talk*.

I must take a diversion here to notify you that the Magliozzi brothers won the PETA "Compassionate Mechanics" Award for looking out for dogs for almost thirty years through, as the award reads, "their (occasionally) sage advice, poignant suggestions, and random speculations."

The brothers won the award because they are *real* "dog people." They frequently mention their staff dogs, Zuzu Berman and Chloe Mayer, on the air; support the use of doggie car seats and other devices to protect traveling animal companions from injury; and are on the lookout for the needs of older dog passengers. They warn of the dangers of driving around with a dog in the back of a pickup truck and of antifreeze poisoning—the taste of antifreeze is attractive to dogs, but its consumption is absolutely fatal. They also ask why, since air bags save human lives, couldn't dogs' lives be saved with "doggie bags?"

Click and Clack also sensibly and sensitively recommend going out and getting another car if your dog is scared of riding in your current vehicle, never putting your dog in charge of guarding your lunch, and—my absolute favorite from their endless repertoire of animal-friendly offerings—Tom points out that "making leather seats involves removing skin from a cow, who presumably had other uses in mind for that skin."

All right, back to the book.

The easy rules are to let dogs be dogs—if they want to sniff each other, grand; it's none of our business.

It is impolite to call dogs "it" like furniture. They are properly addressed as "he" and "she."

Baby talk is also encouraged!

This is the dogs' party and they'll bark if they want to, dig if they want to, roll on their backs if they want to. As has been remarked, "The true essence of friendship is to make allowances for another's lapses."

They'll also sit where they want to. Be thankful you are not a certain Mrs. Albo, who wrote to me from New York to say that she has learned the hard way that it is for *her* to fit in, not for her dogs to make do. She has also learned that the answer to the joke, "Where do you let a ten-ton elephant sleep? Anywhere he wants to!" applies to Chihuahuas, who have the uncanny ability to gain strength in their legs and push you out of bed in the middle of the night if they feel like it. Here is what happens:

"I sleep with four Chihuahuas and each one has her spot on my body. One must be between my arms and tummy on my left.

Let's Have a Dog Party!

Another behind my knees on the right side, one right under both feet, and the last one on my right shoulder. It's a bit chaotic, but as soon as the light goes out they take their positions and go to sleep and then I'd better not budge.

"If I get up in the middle of the night, they all maintain their positions and I have to maneuver my way to fit the spots exactly as they were. Every night without fail it's the same scenario."

Now that's the sort of party guest a dog appreciates!

Warn migraine sufferers that a dog party is not the sort of sedate and peaceful affair that one might expect in a library. Ideally, it will be really, really noisy. Just as when I hear the people whooping it up and singing at the top of their considerable lungs onboard the party boats that sail past our office on the Elizabeth River in Norfolk, Virginia, I figure the louder the music and caterwauling, the more fun the revelers must be having. So it is with a dog party: the louder and wilder the barking, the better the party!

If it reaches the point where you can't hear Animal Control banging on the door because of all the clamor, tail thumping, and yipping, consider your dog party a whopping great success.

If your noisy dog party is held at home, your neighbors will just have to put up with it or go to the movies: It's a party, for goodness' sake! You might even buy them the tickets.

Be discreet when you eat. It is impolite to eat in front of a salivating dog or to reprimand him for drooling. Dogs should always be served first, as their self-control and salivary glands demand it. Remember that nasty animal experimenter Pavlov who rang a bell to signal an impending food delivery? When the dogs started drooling in anticipation, Dr. Pavlov didn't deliver. *We* would never be so mean. Drooling is an innate condition and dogs can't help looking forward to eating. We are just *lucky* we don't drool! (Actually, people *do* drool. When my friend Christine was training for a marathon, she was asked out on a date by a very handsome and charming Navy cadet. Too exhausted to stay awake at the movies, Christine was horrified to wake up and find she had drooled all over her date's arm.)

Cut off any conversation that includes the words "she's so spoiled" or "if only *I* had it that good." We *are* spoiled and we *do* have it that good.

Some rules are more complicated. For example, Chicago resident Debbie Leahy's dog Mugsy refuses to go outside unless she is the first one out the door. If a visitor who is unfamiliar with the protocol lets out one of the other dogs of the household, say Rusty, first, Debbie has to call Rusty back in so that Mugsy can assume her position of "top dog" by being first out the door. Guests must be told.

Party hats should not be worn by adult humans or dogs of any age. Most dogs hate most hats (think: mail carrier, police officer).

Presents are welcome but are not the key (but see Chapter 6).

Hugs, scratches behind the ears, kisses, and tummy rubs are welcome at any time unless your dog becomes too overwhelmed by it all—in which case, back off!

So, now that we've got the rules licked, let's sink our teeth into the other important bits of party business.

4 *Party* PARTICULARS

"Friendship favors no condition
Scorns a narrow-minded creed,
Lovingly fulfills its mission,
Be it word or be it deed."

—*From* The Book of Virtues

When sending out invitations, do be very specific about party etiquette, any party rules (see Chapter 3), and your suggestions as to what, if anything, a guest is encouraged to bring.

If you're having a pool party or a park party (discussed in the next chapter), you may wish to ask guests to provide a towel to dry their dog and a cover for their car seat, and suggest that they dress down.

On the invitation, be clear, too, that, at this party, the *dogs* will rule! There will be no reprimands, harsh words, or other improprieties and no horrid accessories to ruin their day (meaning that any Attila the Hun or Marquis de Sade dog owner types should stay at home, use their shock and pronged collars on themselves, and try barking orders at the furniture).

Let guests know in advance what to expect if your party is outdoors and it rains. You don't want to have to field calls and have people show up to find that the party has been canceled. It is always good to think ahead.

Invitation Ideas

Invitations can come from you or from you and your dog. You can "sign" your dog's name with a paw print, of course, and a photo of him, even a small one, will make a cherished invitation.

Sending e-vites saves time and allows you to pick all sorts of fun images from the Web, including very funny photos of dogs with more tennis balls stuck in their mouths than seems possible or resting in odd positions in front of electric fans, for example, or ones of dogs who are so dear that your heart melts instantly.

Artist Jacquie Lawson's aging mixed Labrador inspired her to come up with a whole selection of e-cards that people go wild over and that are especially appropriate for seasonal and holiday dog parties. See her designs at *www.jacquielawson.com*.

You might also visit the dog section of *www.bluemountain.com*—turning a blind eye to the ones that are not dog respectful—or choose one from *www.funnydog.com*.

Lots of stores and online shops sell attractive party invitations shaped like dog bones. These are also easy and fun to make yourself by cutting out dog bone or paw shapes from hard card or card stock, which comes in various colors at any art store. People seem to like fire hydrants, although I never have. To me, that's like putting a picture of your toilet on an invitation. But it takes all tastes, and along the same lines, "doggie hygiene" bags can be used as invitations, containing directions or instructions, and guests can be asked to return the bag with treats inside them! Of course, invitations with happy dogs on them are a snap to find. Or you might hand deliver—or box up and mail out—small white rubber balls or rubber dog bones with all the dog party details magic-markered onto them or contained on a jolly-looking stick-on label.

If your party has a theme, a whole world of other ideas opens up. For a Mexican-themed party, for example, you can paste Mexican village scenes or señors or señoritas in colorful costumes cut out of travel magazines or free travel brochures onto hard card. You could do the same for a Hawaiian theme. The imagination, like the free-spirited hound, knows no bounds. For an easy-as-pie example, turn to page 196.

Human Guest Favor Bags

If you have human guests, you might end the event with a flourish by giving them some little thing to take home—from your dog, of course. I suggest making it simple and memorable, a useful little whatnot they can pop into a pocket. My favorite: Blizzard's Bone's tiny tins of breath mints. The tins are collectible, and anyone lucky enough to have a Blizzard's Bones tin, like the Un-Bull-ievable or the Loved Lab or the Hot Dog summer tin, will use them to store paperclips or earrings for years to come.

You can order them at *www.blizzardsbones.com*. Because the mints are sugar-free, everyone can share them with their dogs. Or, get them their own. May I suggest "Buddy Biscuits," molasses treats with a hint of mint? They are available from *www.waggin tails.com, www.handsnpaws.com,* and *www.pawstogo.com.*

Put Your Dog in the Picture

There are lots of reasons to memorialize your party by taking photographs. They will make you hug your dog every time you come across them; your dog opening a gift bag is a great opportunity to capture a special moment on film! Pictures of your doggie guests can also be a godsend to their people to use as their own dog party invitations later on. You can post the best of all the photos you and your guests take on a Web site. Two tips from professional dog photographers: Get down to dog level when photographing or you'll miss the best bits of the dog; and try to avoid having a tree sticking out of the back of your dog's head (unless that's the look you are going for).

Keep a Guest Book

It's a good idea to set out a guest book to let humans record their favorite moments and other remarks. You can add photographs, muddy paw prints, and all sorts of mementos. The guest book will make a wonderful journal to reread as your dog ages and a priceless treasure when your beloved dog leaves you to "party with the angels."

An All-Purpose Party Accessory

If your dog doesn't object to wearing a bandana (and most dogs think of a bandana as a soft collar and recognize the extra wolf-whistles they get because they look special in them), you can out-fit him with a special, very handsome cotton batik bandana from *www.pet-bandanas.com*.

The Guest List

Dog parties are unique because, while you may certainly invite your friends and your dog's friends, it is worth remembering that the only guest you really need at this party is . . . yourself. The expression "two's company" describes exactly how most dogs feel. In 999 out of 1,000 cases, a hound would be happiest, a pointer most pleased, if the rest of the world spontaneously combusted, leaving just the two of you alone together, forever.

That said, of course you can invite guests to your dog party, *as long as your dog really likes them all*, because the whole point is for your dog to have fun.

Humane officer Stephanie Bell tells me that her dog, Jasper, knows when visitors are coming and wonders what she does to tip him off—or whether he understands her conversations on the phone.

"It's uncanny," she says, "but about an hour before any guest's anticipated arrival, he becomes increasingly restless. He watches the door and looks out of the windows attentively, barks at every little sound, and makes it very clear that he, too, is expecting somebody."

If you are inviting other dogs to your dog's party, may I suggest that you specify that any other dog guests must be known to be good socializers. The last thing you want is an unneutered, aggressive type fighting with the other guests at your dog's party. Also a little bit bothersome is a dog who has not been adequately advised about lifting his leg on unfamiliar furniture.

Put yourself in your dog's place and imagine who *she* would invite. Don't leave off your guest list anyone, canine or not, whom your dog might still miss since they moved away or changed dog parks some time back. Dogs have long memories. It is extra sad for them to suddenly not see a friend, given that we are ignorant of their language and cannot tell them why we divorced, that Rita moved to Oklahoma, or that that nice guy Sam went off to college. Sometimes a dog party invitation can provide just the perfect prod to bring old pals back together in a joyous reunion of wagging tails.

Are there any siblings you can reunite your dog with, or old dog pals who have gone elsewhere? For instance, dog expert Jayn Meinhardt reports that her neighbor had a large, quiet three-year-old dog named Callie. Says Jayn, "Callie was a very sedate dog, which is why I was so surprised when I looked out the window one day and there was Callie bounding and leaping with another dog. She was running and jumping and yipping and carrying on. I couldn't imagine what she was doing; it was so out of character for this dog.

"When I saw the neighbor a few days later, I asked her about Callie's odd behavior. She explained that her brother had adopted Callie's sibling and moved away. The two dogs had not seen each other in three years, since they were two months old, yet they immediately reverted to the way they had played with each other all those years ago."

Party Prep

Visit *www.tearcatcher.com/animal.html* for the "Party Animal" Dog Celebration Kit, which contains dog toys, doggie invitations, disposable dog bowls, dog treats, a dog tunes CD, and some aromatherapy spray that you can use as a bathroom freshener (but do not put anywhere near the dog). The kit sells for about $20.

Did you know that there are gift registries for dogs? From dog blankets to dishes to overnight bags, your guests can check out what's on your dog's wish list at *www.findgift.com*. For other gift ideas visit *www.pamperedpuppy.com* or *www.room-candy.com*.

And be gracious: If your dog's best friend seems to be the homeless man who sits on the bench in your park, go on, invite him too. Strangers may turn out to be angels, testing your capacity for mercy and tolerance. Even if he doesn't come, you know in your heart that if your dog had control of the guest list, she would want him there.

5

Location, Location, LOCATION: Home, Turf, or Surf

"The reason a dog has so many friends is that he wags his tail instead of his tongue."

—*Anonymous*

There are almost as many factors to consider when choosing a dog party location as there are when choosing a house. For home designer Jean Martin's dog, Tazzie, who likes to carry toads around the backyard in her mouth, a country venue would be best. Jean rescues the toads and has never found one injured. She says, "Tazzie carries these toads even though they secrete a substance that makes dogs foam at the mouth, but she doesn't seem to care."

For the "where" of it all, bearing your dog's personality in mind, you might include these on your list of considerations for potential locations:

- comfort
- space
- convenience (e.g., how much swamp muck are you willing to clean out of the inside of your car afterwards if you throw the dog party in a state park? I'm not saying you shouldn't; I'm just raising the issue.)

East, West, Home Is Often Best

The best place to have a dog party is where your guest of honor will feel most able to enjoy herself, a place where she is able to relax, if that is the nature of the beast, or romp wildly if she is more of an outdoorsy, mushroom-foraging, hill-climbing, ears-out-the-Jeep-window type. In other words, she is the belle of the ball and the one who must have the most fun at the "do" you are putting on just for her. Her temperament should help you choose the setting.

For "Nervous Nellies" like corporate liaison Matt Prescott's dog Simon—who knows full well that Matt is just trying to mask those thunderclaps when he plays Elgar's "Pomp and Circumstance" at decibel levels that could shatter glass—this means as close to the family hearth as possible. In other words, Home, USA.

And at home, the guest of honor can simply go to bed, or crawl under it, if he finds the whole affair has tuckered him out.

Of course, you also might enjoy having the party at home. You get your own kitchen to bake or reheat the food, you are already there without getting the car out of the garage, and perhaps you, too, can slip off to bed if the excitement wears you out.

If you do have the party at your house, scrutinize the scene to see if things that your beloved dog can't reach, isn't interested in, or never knocks over, should be removed for safekeeping. Larger or friskier dogs, or a whole pack of them, are about to make landfall at your place, and you want to be prepared.

While your place might be the best place, do consider a park, a beach, and other venues of interest.

Park It Right Here

I well remember when federal parks started to crack down on dog visitors. We had arrived at the entrance of our favorite park: two humans and three dogs of varying sizes and temperaments but with a single aim—to run and jump about as we had in the past. Then we saw it: the shiny, new, unwelcome (and unwelcoming) sign that read, "No Dogs Allowed." Of course, it's fair enough to keep hounds at bay, given that there's only so much ground to go around for all the deer and small mammals and birds and other species trying to stay alive in the face of human encroachment, but we were crushed.

Luckily, not far from this national park, we found a Virginia state park where we were all able to go boating on the lake in our blow-up dinghy, and run about in the picnic area like actresses in a shampoo commercial.

There are other pleasant park surprises too. Some cities have responded to petitions from citizens' groups with names like "You Gotta Have Park" and "Let Rover Rove!" who have managed to secure a bit of urban real estate for use as dog parks, sometimes even for separate parks for large and small dogs. If your city hasn't done this, get cracking! Mobilize!

So first check your area parks for dog party possibilities. In some, you may need to file a simple form in order to secure a private party permit, but that can allow you to reserve, say, a whole picnic area for your party and your party alone.

Then there are community dog parks. In Norfolk, Virginia, PETA has opened the Bea Arthur Dog Park on the river next to its office. It is complete with a ramp to allow dogs who have jumped into the drink to retrieve balls and tuggies to clamber ashore again and shake themselves off all over the admirers who have gathered to urge them on.

This park is a very popular dog party venue, and office workers next door are used to looking up from their paperwork in the afternoon to see a giant doggie treat cake being handed over the gate and two dozen hungry dogs dashing in its direction. It is also a very popular pickup place for the unattached, or recently detached, dog guardian. (There are even Web sites, like DateMy Pet.com, that have sprung up to celebrate dog park romances.)

Face it, there is nothing more endearing than seeing dogs rolling and running and having a blast. They make you smile, and then the person next to you smiles—although, I can certainly think of a few better pickup lines or conversation starters than, "Do you happen to have an extra plastic bag?"

PETA has provided metal lawn furniture (yes, love seats) in its park, although the only love of *that* kind that's in the air is between the hominids—there is a spay/neuter requirement for the dogs. So far, two weddings and a wedding breakfast have been held by special permission in that park, with dog guests in attendance at all of them, particularly around the food. At one, a dog was "best man." His bow tie looked smashing.

Ask your local humane society, dog rescue group, and veterinarian's office staff what dog parks you and your dog chum(s) may have missed. Although you may frequent the dog park nearest your home, there could be other, bigger, quieter ones worth sniffing out.

Partying in a park does allow you sufficient room to play some of the more vigorous party games suggested in this book. For example, it allows you to throw balls without breaking the china. And, if it's *that* kind of park and you can get away with it, lots of dogs like to use the children's slide, on your lap or independently!

Dog park directories are out there. Arlington, Virginia, has one at *www.arlingtondogs.com* and there are "Dog Lovers' Guides" to various states or metropolitan areas. Check out *www.dogpark .com* and *www.dogster.com*, too, or visit *www.dogfriendly.com* for off-leash sites and other useful information.

Of course, be prepared for party gate-crashers in any public area. While studies show that dogs understand a lot of spoken English without being taught, they still can't read a "Private Party" sign. And it isn't fair to tell dogs who weren't lucky enough to be invited that they are not welcome to sink their teeth into the cake and wrap their tongues around the toys. Let 'em in!

Let's Go to the Beach

If dogs were given their druthers or the handle end of their leashes, I think most of them would choose to spend a day at the beach!

Beaches are meant for dogs. "Keep Off" signs should not be directed at collies any more than at crabs (unless they mean keep off the dunes, a sign we must all obey or there will one day be no beach). If you are prepared to cope with sand and spray, with dogs drinking salt water and then chucking it up at you, and with grit in your sandwiches from the dogs trying to dig their way to China, a beach can be the perfect off-season venue for a dog party.

Just as cats are professional bird watchers, many dogs are professional fish watchers. My friend Linda Tyrrell's dog, Plenty, was one of those dogs whose whole "party" could consist of staring into the water, mesmerized by the possibility of a minnow swimming by and driven insane with ecstasy if a minnow *actually* swam by. A school of them or the shadow of a bigger fish would cause Plenty's heart to burst with excitement.

If Plenty had a wish or a verse in her head it would have been these lines from E. V. Knox's lovely poem "At the Water Zoo":

> Today I have seen all I wish
> For I have seen four thousand fish,
> Inscrutable and rum . . .

Unfortunately, one day Plenty got so excited that she followed a school of fish and got carried away, literally. There was a rather large drainage pipe sticking out of one side of the small island and Plenty was sucked into it. She surfaced after a minute or two, having gone all the way through to the other side quite quickly. Luckily, although she may have emerged a bit dimmer, she seemed as happy as ever.

> "She loves the beach, and she loves to run down and splash in the water, but then when she settles down, we just walk for miles on the sand. She is also my 'border patrol.' She will work hard to keep seagulls, dogs, and people away from me!"
>
> —*Kelly Fidler, accountant, talking about her dog, Ellie*

Another dog I met once on a beach in Cancún was a rock fetishist. And I've met more of those kinds of kinky dogs since.

Rolf, a husky mix, discovered rocks—pebbles actually—rolling in with the surf and, from what I could see from my deck chair, was in the habit of spending approximately all day (slight break for lunch at the cabana) standing in the shallows, digging them out of the sand, losing them to the outgoing wave, and going after them again with vigorous digging when the next wave threw them back. Now and then, Rolf would bark at them hysterically, then go back to his happy hobby, a sort of liberated Hercules trying fruitlessly to clean out the Aegean stables.

Jean Martin's dog Tazzie may hold the clue as to why some dogs are mesmerized by water. Tazzie sits on Jean's bed and stares at her reflection in the mirror for long periods of time. Says Jean, "Where we used to live we had a small pond in the backyard and she would stand in it literally for hours, staring into the water." A canine Narcissus?

Some Hazards to Look Out For

As you may know, the term "dog days" refers to the period from the first days of July through mid-August when the Dog Star, Sirius, rises in the sky and is in conjunction with the Sun. This is when it is the hottest, although with global warming you can cook your breakfast on the roadway as early as June in some summers. Be careful that the sand isn't too hot for your dog's paw pads, which are sensitive. Provide lots of shade under an umbrella and lots of cool fresh water, as salty seawater will make a dog feel queasy. Watch out, too, that your dearest does not burn her feet on the asphalt walkway between beach and car or in the parking lot.

Be sure also to check beach rules and regulations, as many do not allow dogs during those hot summer months, their busiest times of the year. Check with lifeguards or local marine experts before going down to the sea. That way you know to keep dogs out of the water if there is the slightest danger of a riptide, strong currents, or an undertow. No dog's muscles can compete with the ocean's strength when it wants to move in a direction your dog may not wish to go.

A life vest is always proper dress for a sea-going dog or even one doggie-paddling around Lake Placid. I read a little blurb in an English newspaper about a young girl who was swept out to sea on an inflatable lobster, only to be rescued by a man on an inflatable set of dentures! Yes, you read that right. Rescues are unusual enough as it is, so don't take chances, even if you have a giant inflatable dog bone handy.

Let's Party at the Pool

The Swim Center in Rockville, Maryland, is one of the wonderful pools that allows dogs to party *at* the pool and even *in* the pool on the very last day of summer. They "card" the dogs for proof of a rabies vaccination and hit up their guardians for $5, but what a treat! To learn more, visit *www.rockvillemd.gov* and click on "Recreation." It is worth checking with your local pool to see if they have any such arrangement; although, if they have, don't let that mean you will wait until the end of summer to throw your party. Also, if your local government hasn't opened the pool to "hot dogs," you might gather dog guardians together and start lobbying now in time for next year.

A Cautionary Note

If your dog goes in for a dip, silly as this sounds, always check to make sure there's a way for her to get out. Dogs have been found treading water in rivers and canals to the point of exhaustion and sometimes beyond. These days, concrete walls have replaced almost all natural exits from our waterways, and a dog who plunges enthusiastically into the water may face a steep or impossible climb out again.

There are lots of other ways for dogs to get in the swim. If you don't have a cooperative municipal pool or have a pool yourself or access to one, plastic wading or "kiddie" pools are great for dogs, being cheap and easy to acquire and just as much appreciated as the cement number.

Pools aside, a quick look at a good area map for blobs of blue may surprise you. You might find rivers, streams, lakes, a reservoir perhaps, or other bodies of water you hadn't considered or known of before. Before you know it, your formerly landlubber dog will have webbed feet like those Chesapeake Bay retrievers.

6
Selecting and Suggesting
PARTY GIFTS

"She knows the names of all her toys. There is Bear, Banana, Skunk, Broccoli, Dinosaur, Mouse, Hedgehog, Baby Hedgehog, Frog, Violin, and Squirrel."

—Schoolteacher Stephanie Wood, talking about her dog, Chrisette

Everyone loves presents, and dogs are no exception! Writer Donna Zeiber's pug, Sophie, loves her toys so much that she can't bear to let them out of her sight. Every night, without fail, when everyone is safe in bed, she sets off around the house, collecting them all. Then she tucks them, one by one, under the covers between Donna and her husband, Jason, before crawling into bed herself. Donna and Jason say, "Sophie can't sleep unless she's put all her 'babies' to bed!" By noon, all the babies are scattered around the house again as Sophie plays with them all day long.

Some years ago, *Glamour* magazine conducted a poll and found that the vast majority of respondents buy their dog a present over the holidays and/or for their dog's birthday, and 55 percent of those who celebrate Christmas hang a Christmas stocking for their dog and stuff it full of things like squeaky alligators and cookies. My question—and their dogs'—is, "What is wrong with those *other* people?!"

You know the adage, "Give and ye shall receive"? Well, not that a dog's love isn't enough in and of itself, for it is, but remember for a moment that having a dog around helps reduce your stress and can be more reassuring in difficult times than even a human sweetheart.

At the State University of New York at Buffalo, researchers with time on their hands, coupled with a fat grant from a dog food company, studied 240 couples, half of whom had dogs at home. The researchers came to the rather obvious conclusion that "a dog in the home is more effective in controlling psychological reactions in stressful situations than other conventional approaches."

I'm not sure what the "other conventional approaches" are, but they can't possibly be anywhere near as rewarding as getting your mental equilibrium from seeing that wagging tail greeting you at the door or feeling the warmth of a paw on your lap.

Thanks to the dog party you are about to throw, you can return the favor.

Dogs who think their people are, to quote Cole Porter, "a Bendel bonnet, a Shakespeare sonnet," are quite grateful to their people and more than pay them back when the need arises. In some cases, dogs have gone to the point of heroics. Tales of "doggie derring-do" are often in the news. On the television show *Emergency 911*, directed by Arnold Shapiro and starring William Shatner—both very dog friendly—we met a poodle mix who actually saved the day by speed-dialing 911 when her person fell and lost consciousness.

Then there are Rosie, Tina, Athena, Joe, and Ginny—five among thousands of mutt heroes who have saved their sleeping families from fires (one is not allowed to contemplate that perhaps the dogs just wanted a human awake enough to open the door so that *they* could get out). And there's Dan, a dog who pulled a twenty-one-month-old girl from the backyard pool into which she had fallen. There are many more, but you get the idea.

Bag It! Presents for Dog Guests and the Dog of Honor

For a bit of extra fun, you might think about not only what gifts are given, but also how they are presented. You might consider providing one basket, soft bag, or paper grocery bag per dog and popping the collected toys and treats into it. Then, at the right time, the dogs can each be given their personal gift packs. It is terrific fun to see dogs opening (that is, tearing into) their own presents and removing their treats.

Here are some suggestions for what can go into the bag:

- Treats like soy "pigs' ears" (www.petamall.com)
- Dog cookies (see Chapter 10 for recipes)
- Dog cake (see recipe on page 161)
- Squeaky toys like the Shark Dog Toy from Tail-Waggers (www.tail-waggers.com)
- Toys that laugh, like the Chuckle (www.tail-waggers.com)
- Nylabones, Gumadisks, and Fabric Frisbees (www.future pets.com)
- The Humunga Tongue, a giant rubber chew toy that looks really silly sticking out of any dog's mouth, but particularly small dogs' mouths (www.petamall.com)
- Plush toys (It is impossible to overrate plush toys. New Yorker Elaine Sloane's dog, Teddy, a springer spaniel from a rescue group, will not let "Bunny," his plush toy rabbit, out of his sight.)
- Tug toys
- Old clothes or household linens to tear apart

- Socks! (Carpe sockem! Seize the moment to discard all the family's holey ones and put them to interesting use—you can tie them together like the cartoon fire escape rope made from bed sheets, and use them as a tug toy. Don't wash them first if you can bear it.)
- Airline-size blankets (As Coco Chanel said, never underestimate the power of the perfect little wrap. Many dogs, perhaps insecure over early separation from their mothers or a harsh "first owner," have blanket obsessions. Writer Jen O'Connor's bulldog, Punch, had a "blankie" that he sucked on his whole life until it was soaking wet and shredded. He couldn't sleep without it. Her other dog, Maxx, has a different blanket obsession: He can't fall sleep unless his blanket is tucked all around him. And that's true for other dogs, too, like vegetarian campaigner Lindsey Twombly's dog, Elvis. Elvis is only able to sleep when he is tucked into his Ninja Turtle cartoon blanket—he is very adamant about having his "binky.")

Fair Trade

You can buy various kinds of Fair Trade merchandise for dogs if you look for it. Fair Trade means that impoverished workers receive more of the sale price and that the goods are produced with a mind to sustainable development. See *www.fairtrade.org* for more info. Shops like *www.thebigbadwolf.com* offer holistic remedies, Fair Trade toys, and faux fleece beds.

Out of the Bag!

Not all presents are right for putting inside a treat bag, but here are other presents to provide and/or suggest, should a guest ask what to bring (and you feel comfortable enough making a suggestion):

- Pet supply store coupons (The best dog people do not darken the doors of "pet" shops that sell animals, as most come from hideous "puppy mills," where dogs are kept in wire hutches as breeding machines. Patronize only pet supply stores.)
- Coupons for tummy rubs and extra long walks (see page 197 for other suggestions)
- Dog beds, mats, and throws
- A rubber massage mitt
- A doggie massage book
- Portable/collapsible water bowl for hiking
- Doggie vitamins
- Dog sweaters
- Dog videos
- Dog CDs
- Harnesses (far better than a collar—no more tugging on that fragile neck, and less arm strain too!)
- Kazoos, panpipes, and other instruments dogs can howl to (Dogs may be a bit too musical sometimes. Bert, a basset hound, baffled his guardian, corporate liaison Matthew

Prescott, by fleeing into his room when Matt's roommate, Jeremy, played the guitar. Sometimes the guitar sent him running and other times he'd pay no attention. Matt couldn't figure it out. Then one day Jeremy was tuning the guitar and the mystery was revealed. As soon as Jeremy struck the E chord, Bert ran. Jeremy's playing left something to be desired anyway, so it worked out for everyone in the end that he could only play it sparingly.)

- Gift certificates for a stay in a dog-friendly hotel (The Hotel Vintage Plaza in Portland, Oregon, for example, offers dog mats, dog beds, dog walking and play services, spring water and special meals, and chew toys. It is a terrific retreat if you and your dog want a change of scene. Always check the hotels carefully in advance in case their idea of "dog friendly" does not measure up to your or your dog's expectations. Make sure the words "pets welcome" means in the room with you, not stuck away in a basement kennel. Visit www.vintageplaza.com for more information or www.petswelcome.com for other pet-friendly lodging.)

"We give dogs time we can spare, and love we can spare. And, in return, they give us their all. It's the best deal anyone ever made."

—M. Acklam

Four Stars and a Biscuit

Yes, there's always the La Quinta, and it has breakfast doughnuts your dog will certainly enjoy, but if you want to be posh about it, try these luxury digs, places where a dog can lay her weary head right on the pillow, just like at home. The beds in these swanky joints are large enough to allow you on them, too.

Hotel Vintage Park (Seattle, WA): Total luxury in a hotel that makes the perfect headquarters for visits to local vineyards and wineries. *www.hotelvintagepark.com*

The Mayfair Hotel and Spa (Coconut Grove, FL): They may not let Schatzie into the whirlpool, but you can put cucumbers on her eyelids as she snoozes on the perfect mattress in her private room.

Sassy Moose Inn (Jackson Hole, WY): Dogs of all sizes are welcome to size up the movie stars attending Robert Redford's film festival nearby, chase beep-beeping roadrunners in the hills, or chew on a cowboy boot. *www.sassymoose.com*

Hotel Rouge (Washington, DC): If your dog is outgoing, this "adventurous" luxury hotel located in the heart of the nation's capital, will make him feel special. You and your dog can rub elbows at the hotel's complimentary wine hour. *www.rougehotel.com*

Bretton Arms Country Inn at Mount Washington and the Town Houses at Bretton Woods (Bretton Woods, NH): You can bring your Irish wolfhound mix or a dog of any size to this wonderful retreat where two-, three-, and four-bedroom condos are available for two-night minimum stays (small dogs are accommodated in the Inn itself), country breakfasts await you each morning, and all meals are prepared by the inn's gourmet chef. *www.mtwashington .com/resortlodging/brettonarms.cfm*

Really Big, Lasting Gifts

Planning a dog party allows you to focus on your dog's interests, and that's a good time to think what changes in your home or life might provide her with more kindness every day.

Give them a view. Dogs like nothing more than to be nosey neighbors while sitting comfortably. If you are remodeling your home and do not have a floor to ceiling window in it, perhaps it is time to see if you can call in the builders or buy a DIY book and incorporate one into the existing design. If you rent and your landlord is as unpleasant as a guard dog who has been fed gunpowder, you might put one in anyway. Or you could fashion a ledge or get a bench for your dog to sit on (Just be sure to provide ample space for expansive rumps. If your dog has a derrière like one of Renoir's women, you would not want her rolling off her perch during a nap.)

Let them out for recess. Is it time to hire a reliable dog walker who could take your angel to the park midday instead of having him sit uncomfortably in a crate? (Crates are nothing more than boxes, and dogs, like children, should never be "stored"; trainers who recommend them should spend a day in a crate to see how they like it.) Is it time to break the piggy bank and build that fence?

Add a doggie door. How about installing a dog door? Entrepreneur Bob Chorush's mixed collie Py (named in honor of Reg Pycroft, the dashing airman who got her out of a decrepit animal shelter) used to make her entrances and exits through the cat door, rapidly squeezing her not-too-small body in torturous ways through the small opening in the same way an octopus reshapes himself to squeeze into a tiny "hidey hole" in the coral reef. But Py has become somewhat lazy as she's gotten older. Bob reports that, whereas she used to somehow race through the door to bark at people walking by in the street, lately she lies inside the door and puts as much of her head through it as will fit and barks. Bob says the disembodied barking head is quite a sight from the street.

When librarian Karen Porreca's cocker spaniel, Rogan, got a bit doddery, he took a while to learn how to use his new dog door. His companions, Shandy and Darby, went in and out of it quickly and easily, but not so Rogan. So Karen began by giving Rogan lots of praise and encouragement. Meanwhile, Darby decided he needed a little extra attention too. He took to standing on one side of the dog door, whining and pretending that he, too, had no idea how to use it so that Karen would pay extra attention to him. Luckily, Rogan got the hang of the door and life went back to normal!

Lend a helping hand. If you have a geriatric dog, what about buying a ramp or stairs to make getting on the bed or her favorite chair—and getting in and out of the car—less of an ordeal? There are collapsible, stowable ones; cheap but good-quality ones that are as light as a feather because they are made of Styrofoam; and heavy-duty ones for even the largest, lamest old bodies to negotiate. For the best in lightweight, Styrofoam steps and ramps, try Foam Factory at *www.foamfactory.com*. Almost every pet supply store stocks ramps and stairs, and you can get collapsible "suitcase ramps" from *www.moorepet.com*. It's also worth visiting *www.discountramp.com*, which offers a wide variety of other dog's helper equipment. And while we are talking about geriatric dogs, have you provided enough foam pads to keep your dear old friend off the floor and away from drafts? Something soft for her old bones?

> "I have just had the hotel redecorated. Kids will put their dirty handprints on the white walls, stand on the sofas in their dirty shoes, and scream and run around and disturb other guests. I have decided to say no to kids. I don't have a problem with dogs . . . dogs are always welcome in my hotel."
>
> —*Austrian hotelier Roland Ballner*

Buckle up your buddy. Don't curl your lip or turn up your nose at the idea of a car seat, car bed, and/or a safety belt. My beloved Ms. Bea loved going out in the car and always insisted on sitting in the front seat. You could put her in the back seat, but unless you had the strength of ten strong men, you could not keep madam in the back. I didn't worry because—fatal flaw— I fancy myself a really good and really safe driver. (I grew up in India, where there are no lanes and no speed limits on most busy roads, including narrow mountain passes; it's just a mass of cars, scooters, and other vehicles like bullock carts, horse carriages, and big transporters all vying for a wide-open space and using their horns as knights of old might have used a lance.)

Of course the day came when the man in front of me decided to try to take a speck out of his eye *while driving,* slammed on the brakes—perhaps because he found the speck was a shiny quarter, I don't know—and I rear-ended him. Ms. Bea lurched forward and hit her head on the passenger side dashboard.

I'm sure she suffered a nasty headache, because she never, ever would ride in the front seat again. If I glanced at her in the rearview mirror, she was invariably peering forward, trying to make sure I didn't misbehave.

Other Bits and Bobs

Here are some ideas for presents that will come in handy and enhance your dog's pleasure in life, or at least his chances of living a long and healthy life:

- Driving goggles that keep debris out of a dog's eyes
- A life jacket for the water-going dog
- A spa treatment
- An illuminated harness or collar for night jogging
- A doggie companion from the pound (you save a life, gain an extra pal, and eliminate your dog's dull moments in one philanthropic swoop)

I'm not the only one. I don't want to regale you with horror stories, but I do want you to know it isn't just me. There is a certain person I know whose name shall not be mentioned, but who is a Florence Nightingale to dogs, taking in the sorriest of the lot

Let's Have a Dog Party!

and babying them back to health and a sense of security. One little dog she adores—we shall call the dog "M"—used to ride loose in her SUV. The woman-who-shall-remain-nameless was on her way home one evening, stopped at a light, looked in her side mirror for some reason, and saw there in the crossroads *behind* her, her little dog, M!

Yes, M had leaned too far out of the window. Or, to put it another way, the window had been rolled down too far, and M had tumbled out! Our much-chagrined and very lucky driver did a quick U-turn and scooped a miraculously unscathed M out of harm's way. Had she not glanced in her side mirror, who knows where M would be today? Two good reasons not to put off getting car-safety gizmos for *your* dear dog.

Oddball Everyday "Presents"

There are presents that you must remember to deliver to your dog as part of everyday life. They are the smiles and hugs and kind words that make a dog glow, but don't forget these little life enhancers, too:

Scents: No, not that awful dog perfume that some entrepreneur wants you to buy and spritz onto your dog. Such things should be illegal. I mean give your dog, who has about 220 million olfactory cells to our paltry 5 million, something exciting to smell.

Unfortunately, most of the things dogs like to smell don't go well with the living-room rug or your nostrils (decomposition, bacteria, trash, spilled sour cream, horse droppings, flies, nasty crime scenes—you know the sort of thing). And worse, if they *really, really* like the smell, they want to bring it home by snorting it up and rolling in it.

But there are a few smell treats that you *can* give them as a gift. A visit to Imelda Marcos's shoe closet would be the biggest treat of all, but if you don't know her, your own will do. The same goes for the socks that make excellent fodder for a "drag hunt"—sleep in the socks the night before you use them, and then trail them along the ground and hide them somewhere. Or how about collecting some old shoes (from yard sales, the basement, or that pair of tennies you can't get white in the wash any more) and presenting them, preferably on a lawn, to your dog to stick his snout into? And don't get all Felix Unger about your dog not being able to differentiate between "off-limits" shoes and those provided for play. *You* behave! Keep your closet door shut, your "good" shoes on your feet, or just gently remind your pal which are which, should the need arise.

And speaking of lawns, letting a dog roll in freshly cut grass is an easy and cheap delight that she'll deeply appreciate. Keep an eye out in the neighborhood for responsible homeowner activity and take advantage of it. Don't worry if the homeowners look at you peculiarly. They don't want your dog doing certain things *on* their lawn, but surely they won't mind her doing certain other things *with* their lawn. If they do, just ask them if you may please remove the parts of their lawn they were going to throw away. Dogs will roll on grass clippings even if they're redeposited on a different lawn.

A chance to lick the bowl: You know what makes your dog happy, so this is the time to think how you can do more of it. It might be as simple as realizing, as my mother did, that it meant the world to Shawn, our Irish red setter, to be allowed to lick the batter bowl whenever she made a cake or pie.

Your used towel: Amanda Nieves, a catalog manager, has learned to give her dog, Taylor, her towel after she has used it. Ever since he was a puppy, and he's almost eleven now, Taylor has loved to roll in Amanda's towel after she takes her shower.

More Toys!

Here are even more fun toys that any dog would love: The Jolly Pets Romp-n-Roll heavy, non-deflatable handle ball (*www.dogtoys.com*); chewy rope toys (*www.jaxandbones.com*—they also carry very colorful little heart-shaped toys that brighten up any dog's toy chest, and a portion of their proceeds goes to animal rescue groups); a tennis bracelet (four small tennis balls on a tug) and Squirt Ball, which squirts water when chewed (*www.funstuff fordogs.com*); Hol-ee Mol-ee, the "extreme ball for tough K-9s" (*www.petdiscounters.com*); and Kong toys: tough, hardy, a really satisfying chew (*www.kongcompany.com*)!

Amanda says, "He especially loves the towels that I have had my hair wrapped up in after I have washed it. If I hang it on the towel rack to dry he will rub up against it, snorting, for about ten minutes. If I drop it onto the floor he will do a head dive onto it and roll around all over it, snorting the whole time. I don't know why he likes it so much, but he gets very excited when he knows I'm getting out of the shower, as he knows he is going to get my towel. It is absolutely the cutest thing you have ever seen!"

Well, I don't know about that, but this towel thing is pretty common when dogs love their people. Librarian Karen Porreca says that her (now-departed) dog Druzhok (which means "little friend" in Russian), not only rubbed against the towel like a cat high on catnip, but also against her long wet hair if he could.

Permanency: Here's a telling tale: My friend Jayn was telling me about hearing a little boy screaming, "Daddy don't go!" When she got nearer, she watched as the child screamed these words over and over, throwing himself in front of the car in which his father sat, looking pretty upset himself.

Jayn imagined that "Daddy" must be going off with another woman, leaving the home for good, because the little one's screams and tears were so powerful. Listening to this, Jayn felt she was about ready to throw herself in front of the car too. Then she heard the child's father saying, "Ryan, I've told you. Grandma is sick, and Daddy has to go and see her. I'll be back on Tuesday, I promise, and I'll call you tonight."

Jayn watched as the man drove off. She said, "Then I saw the look in Ryan's eyes. He didn't look at all convinced and although I knew that this story had a happy ending, I instantly also knew where I had seen that look before. It is the look in the eyes of every dog and cat who has been dumped at a shelter, while they watch their person walk out the door. And not come back. Ever."

A dog is for life.

Call in Those Canine IOUs: This is the perfect time to block out hours on your calendar for just the two of you to drive somewhere with lots of new smells, or find other ways to spend quality time with your dog. These special moments are for walks and tummy rubs, for massages and romps, for rereading the goo-goo part of this book (page 20), and for jumping into the car, rolling down the windows, and driving down the highway with your dog's hair blowing in the breeze like a Hollywood star's. To remind you not to miss such important moments, at the end of this book you will find a set of coupons you can put in your day book or e-calendar or on the refrigerator door. These coupons are just the ticket!

Some "Gifts" Not to Give to a Dog

Aluminum foil and balloons: These should not be given to a dog or left around where he can get to them. If a dog swallows too large a piece of either, he could suffocate or suffer blocked intestines, because they never dissolve.

"Invisible" fencing: Imagine being zapped with an inexplicable jolt of electricity when you step over an invisible line. No wonder dogs are fast becoming nervous wrecks and a high number are now on some sort of tranquilizing drugs. Also ponder what happens when a dog gets caught up in the moment and goes chasing after a squirrel, makes it over the line, and is then unable to return to the safety of his property. Banished, too, should be electric shock collars. I mean, just imagine putting one on a child. You wouldn't. Such a barbaric device does not belong on a dog either. Reprimand anyone you see using one.

"Anti-barking" collars: Likewise, reprimand anyone using one of these hideous devices that belong on obnoxious, argumentative talk show hosts, not on dogs.

A pet shop puppy companion: Most pups in pet shops come from disgusting "puppy mills," where dogs are confined in squalor to wire-floored, elevated hutches, maintained only to be bred and have their puppies removed, shipped, and sold as soon as they are weaned. Never buy animals from pet shops. A companion from a shelter is, of course, another matter, and you can make a shelter dog's day at *www.petfinder.com.*

Spiked or pronged collars: If you have ever seen pictures of how slaves used to be kept in spiked collars, just the sight of one of these atrocities is enough to make you feel ashamed to be human. If a person can't control his dog to the degree that he needs a spiked collar, something's wrong with the individual at the other end of the leash, not with the dog. Dogs need a harness and training and lots of exercise and socialization. If they strain that much, they aren't getting one or more of those three things. It's that simple.

7

Let's Play! Party Games Dogs Love that Only NEED TWO

"Play more, worry less."

—*Anonymous*

Like us, dogs relish life, liberty, and the pursuit of happiness. Dogs, like girls, just wanna have fun. And it doesn't take much to help them find it.

The humor newspaper *The Onion* ran an article entitled simply, "Dog Experiences Best Day of His Life for 400th Consecutive Day!" It was not far from reality. In the silly story beneath the caption, a family dog named Loki reports: "I got to go outside! I got to sniff the bush! I saw a squirrel and I barked at it and it ran up the tree! Then I came back inside! . . ." It goes on to report that Loki will experience the best day of his life "once again tomorrow, when he digs a hole, chews on a slipper, and almost catches his tail." That's really about all it takes to make a dog happy: freedom to see things and run about and have a good time.

Dogs have an inherent sense of play, as anyone knows who has seen a puppy jumping at an imaginary butterfly or whatever it is the pup is after. Play is, of course, also a sophisticated concept as well as a vital tool used by mother and father canids to teach their young some serious lessons about life, like how to survive. Yet, as complicated as the games we devise can be, given dogs' restricted lives in modern human society, it is the simplest of games that can be the most enjoyable for them.

This book is about how effortless it is to make a dog happy. These simple games are all you will ever need, but the list of games you can play is endless. (It's a lot like Mexican food. You may fancy a tortilla, a burrito, or a chalupa, but in the end it's all rice, beans, and lettuce.) You know more than anyone which games your dog most enjoys, so have a ball! Oh, and speaking of which, take a look at the Babble Ball, which squeaks and "talks" to your dog when he squeezes it (available from *www.thewhole dog.org*).

Liberation from That Leash

Barbara Woodhouse, the famous dog trainer known for her high-pitched cry, "Walkies!"—which could shatter glass at twenty paces—was among the first to warn of the dangers of standard dog collars on a dog's sensitive neck. Even mild yanking can cause serious damage, which is why a leash must be used with a harness, not a collar.

Ms. Woodhouse was also anxious to point out that pent-up energy in a dog must be allowed out or it will explode like beans in a pressure cooker. Frustration can lead to anger, and anger can translate into teeth buried in someone's thigh.

Some very simple games allow dogs to express their natural instincts, most important of which is the freedom to run. Romping about exercises their muscles as they would in nature, and it exercises their minds too. It brings a sense of well-being—as evidenced by psychologists suggesting to depressed patients that, in addition to popping Prozac, they buy some sweatpants and take up jogging.

It is tempting to imagine that dogs are happy being sedentary, but Afghan hounds who live in apartments do not lose their natural ability to dash to the top of a sand dune in a flash. And greyhounds and whippets unleashed and pointed in the direction of even a totally rabbitless field have been clocked at over 45 mph, which is pretty impressive by any standard.

Dog observer Sebastian Zoesch says that if you think dogs are couch potatoes, you might take a look at one of the proliferating Web sites of dogs who like to skateboard and snowboard, like *www.realskate.com*. He knows one such demon racer. Tyson is a dog who runs using three paws and pushes the skateboard with his fourth. When he and the skateboard get fast enough he jumps completely on the skateboard and somehow manages to steer it by leaning to one side. You can see Tyson, who, naturally, hails from somewhere in California, in action at *www.fun restarea.com*; click on "dog skating video."

Dig This!

A lot of dogs are closet archeologists. They were born to dig!

PETA staffer Chris Garnett's mother's dog, Emilee, has decided not to have her digging and burying instincts defeated by the fact that the Garnett household has hardwood floors. She takes a biscuit and finds a corner to "dig." She places the biscuit carefully, and then "covers" the biscuit by pushing imaginary dirt over it.

Digging is how a good dog provides a home for her family, in the ground, where it is neither too hot nor too cold. And a comfortable place for a dog to lie down means a depression in the earth, not a flat surface, which is why they are always digging about, rearranging their bedding. A nicely dug hole, every dog knows, is far cooler and comfier on a broiling summer's day than sitting, plonk, on the hot ground.

And dogs, imbued with those sensitive ears, long to investigate the sounds of moles, earthworms, and other moving creatures they can hear underground.

> "She loves gardening and loves to roll large rocks around the backyard with her head to 'landscape' the area. If she sees me plant flowers and shrubs, she will dig them up after I leave and then bring them to me as gifts."
>
> —Jean Martin, home designer, describing the interests of her dog, Tazzie

The beach is perfect for a good dig, as is a freshly dug field where the soil has been conveniently loosened for a good secondary dig. Perhaps you can allot a little space in your own yard where, just like a child's sandbox, it is okay for your dog to dig. You could start the whole thing off with a shovel, then get down on all fours and see where things go from there.

A real sandbox isn't a bad idea either. All you need are some two-by-fours and a few bags of sand from the garden store and you have created the perfect environment for your dog to cast himself as Steve McQueen in *The Great Escape*. If you are lucky, he might find an ancient artifact and make your fortune. Actually, make that *his* fortune.

The Bark-a-Thon

Dogs spend most of their lives listening to humans talking, shouting, singing, laughing, and generally making noise. It is probably as awful for them as it would be for us if we had to listen to hyenas going on every night, baying incomprehensibly, and every time we tried to open our mouths, the hyenas told us to put a sock in it.

And that's what happens. It's "Be quiet!" "Rufus, no!" and "Shush, sweetie, shush!" even when they, with their keen senses, are trying magnanimously to warn us of a smoldering match in the wastepaper basket, a volcanic eruption in a neighboring country, or a salesman coming down the driveway.

You try going without saying anything for what's basically a lifetime!

Writer Kathy Guillermo once told me that she found out that the way to get her dog to stop barking when someone walks past the house or rings the doorbell is definitely not to yell, "Be quiet!" but to go look out the window or door and say, "Thank you, Josie, for letting me know." Josie immediately stops barking and relaxes. As Kathy says, "They don't just bark to drive us nuts, but to communicate a message."

A dog needs to bark just as much as a bird needs to chirp or you need to talk back to Bill O'Reilly when he is saying annoying things on TV.

I hadn't realized how repressive I was being to my old dog, Ms. Bea, until a reporter pointed out to me that her second name seemed to be "quiet!" Luckily, Ms. Bea, a cross between a German shepherd and a couch, a dog with the uppity deportment and demeanor of the Grande Dame in the old Marx Brothers movies, paid me no mind and barked not only when there was someone at the door but whenever she felt like it, which was a lot. Also luckily, my apartment was built a century earlier and the walls were very thick.

It all went sideways when I had to go overseas for a little while. I made the mistake of leaving Ms. Bea in the care of a young woman named Donna. It turned out that Donna had a strange sense of humor. A little while after I left, she decided it would be a hoot if she encouraged Ms. Bea to bark at everything! Her chief modus operandi in this mission was to drive along with the window down and then stop and point out joggers, birds, buses, pedestrians—pretty much anything that moved or didn't—and then get Ms. Bea excited about whatever it was. As soon as Ms. Bea started barking, she would receive mighty praise and a treat.

By the time I returned, I had lost a dog and gained a barking machine. Life was never the same and my favorite fashion accessory soon became earplugs. Ms. Bea never quite got back to her more occasional barking style.

I am not suggesting that you do what Donna did, even for an hour, but a dog, like Pavarotti, needs to give his lungs a good airing once in a while and bark his heart out. I am suggesting that a great treat is to suspend all the rules and let your dog's vocal cords have a field day. Throw all caution to the wind, neighbors be damned!

I'm a Retriever

Many dogs are born retrievers. Take Duke, for example. In more innocent days, years ago, when Web designer Jennifer Huls was a little tyke, her mom and dad used to leave her in the care of Duke, a Great Dane who, luckily for Jen, had great paternal instincts. In fact, Duke turned out to be a more conscientious babysitter than a lot of teenagers, and if Jennifer managed to crawl out of the backyard, Duke would track her down, carry her back to the backyard by her diaper, plop her on the ground, and lie across her legs to stop her from toddling off again.

> "She likes you to play 'Fetch' twenty-four hours a day and when she doesn't get any takers she'll look at you, cock her head to the side, and snap her jaws together like she's barking, but she doesn't make any sound."
>
> —*Campaign manager Megan Hartman, talking about her dog, Cinnamon*

Dogs can enjoy spectator sports, too. The Chicago White Sox let dogs in on the action. They hold "Dog Day" at Comiskey Park, welcoming about 450 or more dogs to sit with their guardians in the right-center-field bleacher seats. So does Prince George's County Stadium just outside Washington, D.C., and many other ballparks nationwide. While I think that's grand, I can't imagine the restraint exercised by the dogs (and the aching arms of the people trying to hold their dogs back every time the pitcher throws the ball). When the man hollers, "Play Ball!" and dogs are present, it seems very rude not to have that invitation extend across species lines.

Retrieving a trophy, such as a ball or stick, is the manifestation of your dog's ancestral desire to bring prized finds back to his pack or satisfies her desire to outfit her den.

Thank goodness for the invention of the little plastic ball-thrower, now available in most pet supply stores and at *www thewholedog.org*. Whoever came up with this arm-saver deserves a Nobel Prize. Also helpful, although you have to bend to reload, is the Ball Stomp'r (from Happy Dog Toys), which allows you to use your foot to propel tennis balls a long, long way.

If your dog seems to have mastered one way of playing ball, try another. Many dogs absolutely relish a challenge. Librarian Karen Porreca's dog, Rogan, could run like the wind. Karen would throw a ball over the roof of the house and Rogan would watch it go, then take off and run around to the backyard as fast as he could to catch it. For the dog who is reluctant to give up the sopping ball after fetching it, have a second one on hand to throw.

It's also good to remind yourself that a dog can run himself ragged. He is so anxious to please and prove himself to his person that he will continue to fetch long after he should have taken a rest. Be your dog's best friend *and* health monitor! Know when to stop.

A Cautionary Note

If you are using tennis balls, check them carefully and discard any that show signs of coming undone—the rubber bands that the best ones are made from can cause stomach impaction that can kill. And make the swap whenever you see any ball being reduced to small pieces. The risk is not worth the wait.

Gimme That Stick (and Throw It While You're at It)

Balls are one thing, but sticks are another. I've watched the tiniest of dogs proudly lugging around sticks that dwarf them.

This game is a version of "Who's the King of the Castle?" because, when more than one dog plays it, it's plain to see that whoever has the stick is boss. You can see your dog smile through the clenched teeth that are holding on to the prize!

It is amazing that dogs don't get more splinters than they do, but as long as you are careful to note any sensitivity of the mouth afterward, and knowing that dogs have been whittling wood with their mouths for centuries, I am in favor of throwing caution to the wind (along with the stick).

In preparation for your party, you might embark on a stick-collecting expedition to the woods or be on the lookout for proper sticks on your regular walks. How surprised your cherub will be when you produce a whole box full of wondrous sticks that he can choose from.

Let's Have a Dog Party!

Tug-of-War

I wonder if dogs imagine they are ripping a carcass apart when they play tug-of-war? Do they realize what this game represents, or is such a thought too far removed from their domesticated experience? Who cares as long as they are having a blast!

Cooking instructor Corey Portalatin-Berrien thinks that her dog, Mantequilla, is having a grand old time when she vacuums the house. Mante doesn't seem afraid of the vacuum at all, but runs up to it, barks at it, takes off running around the house, then returns to pounce on it, picking the front of it up off the ground to play tug-of-war with it. To each dog his own.

Most pet supply stores carry sturdy ropes, but an old towel or pillowcase works just as well. Do be cautious not to pull too hard, as even the toughest dogs' teeth are easily hurt, and be especially careful not to tug too much if playing with a pup or an old fellow.

Task and Reward

This is an obedience school graduation game, and it's a tiny bit tricky as there must be no failure. Go over the directions (not to be called "commands" unless the dog is actually in the military) that your dog knows, such as "sit," "down," "come," "up," and so on. Place some new toys in a chest or other solid container that the dog cannot get into without human assistance. Position your dog at least twenty feet from the toy chest and put him through one of his paces. As soon as he does what he's asked,

Let's Play!

say, "Good boy!" or whatever praise phrase you commonly use, and then lead him to the chest, open it, and let him stick his nose inside and pick a toy. Choosing is a great treat for dogs, as they are often given whatever someone else chooses for them and are not allowed to make any selections. Close the chest after the selection is made and, after a decent interval to allow your dog to play with his new toy, do the whole thing all over again using another direction.

Ghost!

This is not for timid dogs! I first got the idea from my little Chihuahua/fox terrier mix, Conchita. Conchita was found shivering in the snow (a Chihuahua lost in the snow—oh, no!) and had suffered some trauma, so her little frame was bent into a banana-shape. She seemed a pathetic little destitute thing when I picked her up, wrapped her in my cardigan, and took her home.

I was determined not to adopt Conchita, just give her a temporary way station until she found that special someone. But Conchita had moved one too many times and wasn't about to be moved again. She put her cunning plan to make me love her into action.

The morning after her first night, I got ready for work and then stripped the bed and got out clean sheets to remake it. Suddenly, Conchita began bouncing around like a chipmunk, giving me sly little smiles, her lips turned back, making silly play growl noises, and then going into the classical play "bow"—her front legs pushed out in front of her, her backside up in the air, and her stump of a tail wagging. As I flapped the clean sheet to spread it over the mattress, Conchita jumped under it and chased the air as it billowed. How could I possibly not love her?

Conchita's behavior was exemplary. One day, I made up my mind. I said, out loud, "Okay, you can stay," to this smiling little girl. From that moment on, Conchita became a banshee, barking at everyone, biting strangers, and generally asserting the personality that she had so cleverly suppressed while winning my heart. Of course, I loved her dearly until the day she died, some fifteen years later.

The sheet game, which consists only of flapping the sheet over your dog, is adored by many dogs, especially ones small enough to play it on your bed. But you will find that taking a sheet out into the yard or into any open space and flapping it over your dog may create a great new game to love and play. Koro was one such big lummox of a dog who liked to play-bite her other dog pals at home by lurking behind a curtain or a rug thrown over a sofa. Everyone seems to love the sport!

"He has an obsession with sticks that extends to entire tree branches that fall into our yard during a storm. He'll do victory laps around the yard with branches three inches thick and ten feet long."

—Computer specialist Sarah King, talking about her dog, Clyde

Let's Roll

Dogs, especially really small ones, get a crick in their neck (and even compressed discs!) from having to look up at their humans all the time. A dog cannot believe her luck when she finds her human on all fours or, better yet, lying on the ground and ready to roughhouse, or at least roll about a bit with her. There's not much to this, except your willingness to leave the heights of humandom and get down to earth, for your dog's sake. And if you are in the mood for a massage, lie on the ground and it's a good bet that your dog will come and stand on you!

Splish, Splash (No, We're Not Taking a B-A-T-H!)

If you aren't near a body of water that your dog and her chums can enjoy during summer, make your dog party special by re-creating a Water World in your yard. Buy a plastic kiddie pool, or better yet several plastic pools, for the dogs to cavort in, jump in and out of, and generally make waves.

Bring out the hose and prepare to get wet. Even small, old dogs enjoy wading and soaking their paws and cooling their tummies on a hot day.

Find the Bonio

This is the equivalent of a children's Easter egg hunt but with dog treats. Having to seek out buried or hidden food rather than having it plonked down in front of him allows a dog the anticipation and thrill of the hunt that activates his gray matter and makes him feel like more than just an inactive accessory to your life. It also aids digestion by activating the salivary glands and gastric juices and setting up a scenario in which he can satisfy his desire to stock his den.

One of the most beautiful (and sad) books ever written about your dog's cousins, *Never Cry Wolf* by Farley Mowat, contains passages that describe in a most moving way the enormous pride of the wolf parent bringing home food for his family. Bring out the wolf in your dog with this simple game in which you stash the treats in advance, help him find the first one, whisper words of encouragement, and . . . off he goes!

Don't worry that he won't find the treats. Dogs are used around the world to sniff out everything from strawberry-scented truffles to dangerous landmines, from cocaine to termites to deeply buried bodies. Dogs can even detect cancerous tumors by sniffing patients' breath, and, most impressive of all, they get it right more often than we can with our most sophisticated mammograms (88 percent by them; 85 percent by the mammogram).

Your dog may be a hoarder, as was writer Chrissy Matthies's dog Dixie, a beagle she adopted from an SPCA. She has since passed away, but when Dixie was alive she chose underneath Chrissy's pillow as the place to hide all her treasures and rainy-day reserves. One day, Chrissy and her children were feeding bread to ducks outside their apartment. Chrissy was distracted for a few minutes and when she turned around, the bread was gone. That night, she found all the mushy bread under her pillow.

Chrissy says, "Dixie also liked to chew the eyes off her stuffed animals. And guess where she put them? I would frequently lift up my pillow and find plastic eyes staring back at me. It was a little eerie, to say the least."

If, at day's end, your dog has plowed his schnozzle through hard ground, he may need a little nose balm to soothe it. I am not kidding! There is such a thing for chapped noses (it works quite well on human lips, too): Nose Balm from the Well-Adjusted Dog Company is vegan, all natural, moisturizing, soothing, and healing for the dog who dug a little too deep in that parched earth. For details or to order, contact the Well-Adjusted Dog Company by phone at 888-935-5364 or visit *http://thewelladjusted dogco.com.*

"If you think a dog can't count, try putting three dog biscuits in your pocket and then giving him only two of them."

—*Author Phil Pastoret*

Puzzle Party/Mind Games

Just as every dog is an individual, a thinker in his or her own right, so every species has its own type of Intelligence Quotient. Dogs have an innate IQ that you and I could not match if ever we had to find a skier buried under an avalanche, keep a lost toddler warm in a freezing forest, or make our way home after being dropped off in a remote area.

But even the best of minds needs developing and must not be allowed to get rusty. Just ask Terry Waite, who, like so many POWs, devised all sorts of primitive ways, such as practicing arithmetic and trying to remember whole passages of literature, to keep mentally alert while locked on a balcony by himself for several years. Set aside time to have fun with your dog by exploring and exercising her or her psyche.

A Few Toys and Activities to Stimulate a Canine Brain

Noncompetitive games that you and your dog can play together include basic problem-solving skills and can earn your dog ribbons and trophies. Check out *www.dog-games.co.uk.*

The Buster Fun Bone Treat is an extremely hard game in which a dog has to try to extract differently colored bones from a container in order to win an award. This game requires an investment of your time, but the delight of seeing your dog learn more and more is worth every second. Also from *www.dog games.co.uk.*

The I-Cube Puzzle is a plush cube containing squeaking balls that dogs can retrieve from inside it. The Hide-a-Bee Puzzle and Hide-a-Squirrel Puzzle stimulate dogs' minds and play on their curiosity. Available at *www.tail-waggers.com.*

If you learn how to get your dog to use your (or anyone's) scent as a clue to which object to select from a group of objects, you can even amaze your friends by having your dog pick out the card you selected and then put back in the pack. Roy Hunter's amazing book, *Fun Nose Work* will show you how. This book, available from *www.amazon.com* or from *www.dog-games. co.uk,* is full of interesting interactive games that engage a dog's nose and his brain and allow you to play with your dog as you both learn. In this book, Mr. Hunter, who spent twenty-five years working in the dog's section of the Metropolitan Police force of London, England, describes how dogs can be trained to find anything and everything including, in the case of a dog in New Zealand, six-inch nails under six inches of water! He takes guardian and dog through their paces, starting with easy-as-pie lessons to mind-boggling feats of tracking. Everything is done by understanding a dog's natural ability and rewarding progress.

If you want to get serious about training your dog (for his enjoyment and yours), then I suggest reading *Fun and Games with Dogs,* a casually titled but quite serious book also by Roy Hunter. Hunter uses only the dog's own interest to make him a master of useful "tricks," from knowing when to crawl (in a fire or to rescue someone) to being able to drop something (a poisonous material) to walking backward (in a narrow space). A grand book indeed.

"I lived in a house where my roommate had an Akita companion named Delma. Delma would greet me every day in a new, humorous way when I arrived home: She once slithered on her belly, approaching slowly until she got to the door; or she would sit at the door with my toothbrush in her mouth; or she would hide behind a couch and ambush me when I went past. It was so clear that she was deliberately, consciously being creative."

—*Philip Schein, Virginia wildlife enthusiast*

And One Game for You

Here's a pocket game to occupy the adult mind while Rover romps with other dogs. It's called Spot the Dog. This is one of those mesmerizing little puzzles that slips into your pocket and drives you crazy in a heartbeat. It's a little plastic puzzle, like the old puzzles where you had to guide a tiny ball through a maze, only this one makes you move spots around in water to try to cover a Dalmatian. You must get the large spots in the large holes and the small spots in the—you get the picture. Available from Office Playground at *www.officeplayground.com*; type "spot the dog" in the search bar.

Now that you have enough games in mind (and mind games) to ensure everyone's amusement, let's put our gray matter to work on a party theme.

8 *Pick a* PARTY THEME

"I think that every family should have a dog; it's like having a perpetual baby."

—*Dr. John Brown*

There are as many themes for dog parties as a dog has dreams. From the simple to the exotic and from the sublime to the ridiculous, including these:

- Birthday (or Adoption Day)
- Coming of Age Party
- Special Occasion and Once-in-a-Lifetime Parties
- Dog Appreciation Day
- Retirement Party
- Religious-Themed Parties
- Howl-a-Thon
- Car Party
- Boat Party
- Take-a-Hike Party
- Night at the Movies
- Hawaiian Luau
- Mexican Fiesta
- Oktoberfest
- Reunion Party
- Total Relaxation Party

You can make your dog party a home affair or a big bash, a tea-for-two deal or a blowout—it's all up to you. If there is a theme you are particularly drawn to, you can design a party to fit the bill. Here are some themes to think about.

Please your dog (and have a ball) by having them all, and then some, if you can!

Birthday (or Adoption Day) Party

The most obvious party is the birthday party. More than half of *Washingtonian* magazine readers polled said they throw their dog a birthday party, so don't leave this one off your social calendar. If you don't know when your dog was born, your dog is probably a "rescue." Good for you! You can use your dog's adoption date as a sort of "re-birthday" or decide on a birthday date and stick to it every year. You can try your hand at making the cake recipe on page 161, or buy the "yellow cake with icing," which is actually a musical dog toy, available from *www.dogtoys.com.*

Coming of Age Party

This party marks your dog's sterilization day, as there are way too many homeless doggies in the world. In Healdsburg, California, the animal shelter celebrates a "no birth" nation by holding a party, rather saucily called the Spay-ghetti and Dinner. For the humans, there is champagne and popcorn, gourmet "spay-ghetti" and all the fixings. All the proceeds go to help fund low-cost sterilization in their county.

You can do the same or create your own "Neuter Is Cuter" theme. Friends of mine announced an "antilittering" party in the park and asked everyone to donate the proceeds from a group can and bottle collection to help PETA's SNIP (Spay and Neuter Immediately, Please!) mobile subsidized sterilizations. (SNIP has sterilized over 30,000 dogs and cats since it started in 2001.) Local radio stations and newspapers may be happy to advertise your party if it benefits such a worthy community goal.

Special Occasion and Once-in-a-Lifetime Parties

Can you imagine what a fine party the eighty dogs rescued from New Orleans after Hurricane Katrina enjoyed aboard Texas oil magnate T. Boone Pickens's jet as they were transported? They were sprawled out in passenger seats and careening up and down the aisles of the plane to safety, glorious safety. What are you ready to celebrate? A new job? The solstice? Being alive?

A Charity Ball

It can be very la-di-da or as casual as can be. Guests can come in tuxedos and party dresses or in their scuffies and house-coats—whatever you desire. You can drink champagne or sip lemonade out of paper cups, dance in high heels or roll on the ground.

> "My first dog showed up on our doorstep with a note around her neck that read, 'Please take care of me, my mommy won't let me keep her [sic].' She lived to be sixteen with us and slept with a teddy bear that she would wrap her arm around like a little child and snuggle it all night."
>
> —Schoolteacher Stephanie Wood,
> talking about her dog, Breena

The only thing that's important is the idea, and it's great for giving guests a genuinely good feeling. This party takes a page from George Clooney's book. Clooney is not only talented and handsome, but kind too. He once took pity on a potbellied pig who needed a place to lay down his weary trotters, adopted him, and let him live in his own home. And when George lost his beloved dog to a rattlesnake, he described the incident as part of "the worst year of my life."

What's on my mind at the moment is that George donated his Oscar gala bag and all its expensive contents to United Way, which sold the whole kit and caboodle for $45,000. Now, while it is doubtful that most dog party guests would bring diamond-studded collars and bejeweled leashes, caviar and bottles of Jean Patou's Joy that could be put up for auction, party gifts can truly make a dent in a deserving charity's budget or give some "poor" dogs a real boost.

The idea is for every guest to bring to the party a donation for a stray dogs' home, animal shelter, or dog foster care facility, or a bag of balls and other presents for the dogs whiling away their sentences in them.

Guests can go whole hog and involve their offices, clubs, schools, and neighborhoods in the collection of funds or in filling a bag with toys, blankets, chewies, and other delights for needy dogs. One idea is to have everyone chip in to buy dog beds for a local animal shelter. Kuranda Dog Beds has a program that allows you to buy dog beds for shelters at a discount. See *www.kuranda.com*. You might give every guest a Certificate of Appreciation or a thank-you note from the recipients. (For other ways to help needy dogs, see Chapter 14.)

> ## *Certificate of Appreciation to*
>
> _____
>
> for your kind donation to help a needy dog at
> the _____ shelter.
>
> You have made a poor dog rich today!
>
> ## Thank you!

Dog Appreciation Day

No matter what it is about your dog that makes you smile or look at her in wonder, there ain't nothin' like a dog!

Anytime your dog brightens your day, comes to comfort you when you are upset about some horror at work or home, or forgives you your inadequacies with a kiss, declare "Dog Appreciation Day" and throw him a party, if only to read him the loving words on page 20.

Retirement Party

Throw this party when your dog is getting a bit dog-eared and frail. Or when a "service dog" like the wonderful hearing ear dogs, who are all adopted from shelters and stay with the family for life, retires because he or she has . . . gone deaf!

One of the best dog parties I have ever attended was a retirement party for a police dog named Kirk. Kirk was a "throwaway" dog who ended up at the Washington Humane Society/SPCA at a time when I was the society's director of cruelty investigations. The Metropolitan Police Department (MPD) has an excellent and humane training course for dogs; the graduate dogs live with the officers at home when not on duty; and when the dog's days are done he is retired to sit by the officer's hearth (not the case in all police departments, where sometimes dogs are "retired" by being sold to the highest bidder, who may be a junkyard owner). Satisfied that a working dog with the MPD had a good life, if the MPD came looking for a dog, the society obliged.

Kirk worked with Officer Thomas K. Delahanty. In March, 1981, Officer Delahanty was standing with other police officers outside a hotel in Washington waiting for President Reagan to arrive. Kirk hadn't been feeling well and was resting back at Officer Delahanty's home. On that morning, shots rang out, injuring President Reagan, White House Press Secretary James Brady, and Officer Delahanty.

> "He is eighty pounds of pure energy. When my husband, Giehl, leaves for work in the morning, he crawls under the covers, turns around and lies with his head on Giehl's pillow."
>
> —Computer specialist Sarah King,
> talking about her dog, Clyde

Officer Delahanty retired soon after the incident from a disability caused by the wounds he incurred that day. He said that, most of all, he was so glad that the MPD allowed him to retire Kirk, too, even though his dog was not officially ready to retire. Hence, the party, which was held in the Maryland countryside. Attending police dogs not only posed in their guardians' police hats but were allowed to jump into the pool!

Religious-Themed Parties

Mark Twain said that no man's religion is any good if his dog isn't the better for it. I've always thought that dogs were blessed, if you'll pardon the use of the word, with not having to bother with such concerns as nationality, race, and religion. St. John the Divine in New York City and other churches now offer the "Blessing of the Animals." Surely it has a spiritual significance for the human participants; from the dog's point of view, however, I suspect it is just a lovely outing. (For the camels and cats, it's more akin to a miserable and frightening experience.)

If you ever set foot in the Aspin Hill Memorial Park and Pet Cemetery in Silver Spring, Maryland, you will find something remarkable. Almost every grave is decorated with a statue of the Virgin Mary, a menorah, angels, the Star of David, or little statues of Jesus on the Cross. My favorite, however, isn't religious at all. It is the wonderful old lithograph of a spaniel who delivered his guardian's deposit to the bank every day, carrying the deposit book in his mouth. And my favorite epitaph, "To Baby, who is just sleeping," is on the gravestone for a beloved mixed Chihuahua, along with a likeness of her etched in the stone, who did, indeed, look as if she were just sleeping.

One devout Christian, metropolitan Washington resident Donna Brazile, baptized her dog, Chip, before he underwent surgery. She says, "That's how I knew I loved him!" All this goes to show that a lot of people firmly believe that the dogs in their families assume the same religion as the humans.

Dogs are egalitarians. I used to pop into the Salvation Army in Washington, D.C., to buy Ms. Bea the big plastic dolls she loved to carry around with her. Once, a young woman stopped me when Ms. Bea and I were walking down the street, a doll firmly in Ms. Bea's mouth.

"How *dare* you have your dog carry a *black* baby doll?" she screamed at me, clearly livid.

That threw me for a loop. I hadn't ever thought about picking out a doll by *color* before. Ms. Bea was brown but, apparently, in the same way only "Catholic" dogs live in Catholic houses, in this woman's mind Ms. Bea was "white" because I am. And to her that meant Ms. Bea must only be permitted to carry white dolls around.

One of the things I like to celebrate about dogs is their wonderful accepting nature that looks beyond the boundaries their human companions sometimes erect. That is not to say dogs will not learn to fear people who abuse them; a dog abused by a man will quickly learn to fear men in general. But their nature is very different and very, very tolerant.

But enough of that! Let's eat cake! Whatever your religion, your dog will surely enjoy an appropriately themed fest.

How About a Bark Mitzvah?

I was once invited to a "Bark Mitzvah," or Jewish coming of age party, for a dog who was about to turn two, which is roughly equivalent to thirteen years for a human boy. It turned out not to be the last such event.

Lisa Katz, who writes on *www.judaism.about.com*, said, "I almost fell off my chair when I first heard the latest craze among American Jews." She found out that "some people do Bark Mitzvahs for Purim entertainment, some do it to raise money for charity, and others do it simply for the fun of it."

The Miami Herald reported on a Bark Mitzvah held by Edie and Ed Rudy for their thirteen-year-old poodle, Columbo, which won praise and raised eyebrows, particularly at Columbo's get-up: a gold yarmulke and a prayer shawl! And he was presented with a certificate of congratulations signed by Rabbi Rex Doberman of Congregation Beth Poodle.

According to *The Miami Herald* story, Edie, whose children are all grown up, said, "He is like a child." Edie goes on to say, "With so much going on in the world, it's nice to come together and celebrate something positive."

The paper reported that Rabbi Gary Glickstein of Temple Beth Sholom, a Reform synagogue in Miami Beach, appreciates the different ways people find to express their Judaism. "It is easy to make fun of something here," the paper quoted him. "But I think there is a motivation here that is positive in some way."

All Dogs Go to Heaven

A grocer named Muldoon lived in the Irish countryside with his dear dog, Patrick. One day Patrick fell ill. Muldoon went to the parish priest and said, "Father, my dog is ill. Could you possibly be saying a Mass for the poor dear?"

Father Patrick told the grocer, "No, we can't have services for an animal in the church. But I'll tell you what, there's a new denomination down the road and no telling what they believe in, but maybe they'll do something for the animal."

Muldoon said, "I'll go right now. By the way, do you think $50,000 is enough to donate for the service?"

Father Patrick replied, "Now, why didn't you tell me the dog was Catholic?"

You can find all you need for a Bark Mitzvah on the Internet. Bark Mitzvah packages can include Star of David treats and Bark Mitzvah certificates to commemorate the special occasion. For about $50, *www.placeseveryone.com* offers a seating kit for your Bark Mitzvah celebration, as well as a Bark Mitzvah certificate.

There's no need to leave Christian dogs out of the picture, of course. They love a church picnic every bit as much as any saint or sinner. They also love an Easter egg hunt! Now, just as I'm sure not every child on the White House lawn is a card-carrying Christian come time for the Easter egg hunt, I wouldn't examine your dog's faith that closely. The party's the thing.

> "I wonder if other dogs think poodles are members of some weird religious cult?"

> —*Comic Rita Rudner*

All it takes is to buy some of those tiny plastic eggs that come apart and then stuff them full of treats and do them up again. Hide them around the yard or house for your dog to find.

If you'd like to start off the hunt with a prayer, go for it. Some people pray for their dogs and some pray with their dogs; others find their dogs epitomize "good Christian values" and just leave it at that. To read heartfelt prayers from "dog people," may I suggest a visit to *www.belief.net*? Type "dogs" or "pets" in the search bar.

And, finally, let's hear a prayer from Albert Schweitzer, who started the first hospital in Lambaréné in Equatorial Africa, when there was no medical care there at all. He had a great respect for all life and was also a devout Christian. Into his charge and custody came the lame, the sick, and the dying of all species, from children and old people who had been cast out by their villages to pelicans, cats, and donkeys.

Every night since he was a little boy, Dr. Schweitzer knelt beside his bed and added to his prayers for human salvation and God's mercy, this one:

"Dear God, protect and bless all beings that breathe, keep all evil from them, and let them sleep in peace. Amen."

Howl-a-Thon

Howling at the moon, the fire truck, or thin air is a great way to celebrate the evening with your dog. As you look up into the heavens on a clear night—the kind of night ripe for baying at the moon—you may see the Dog Star, Sirius, keeping watch over the arch of the Milky Way. This star is a symbol of power, will, and steadfastness of purpose—all the traits apparent in a really good dog (and, as you and I know, there are no "bad dogs").

To get you primed for a good howl, let me start off with Gaye Berglas telling the story of Lucy, a dog who "didn't just come into our lives, she blew in."

"Lucy was delivered to our home from the shelter, all twelve pounds of her—a whirling tumble of wiry fur, one ear that stood up, one that didn't. She was a bag of bones and all four of her paws were raw from pounding the pavement, looking for scraps. Almost immediately, my husband became her favorite, and she was intent on impressing him and winning his favor. She had decided that this was the place that would give her the love and care she so desperately needed. She was right. Who knew, then, that among her many charms and talents, Lucy could sing—with gusto.

Let's Have a Dog Party!

"We discovered this quite by accident, of course. You never really know what a rescued dog has learned, or can or cannot do, until your lives are shared. It was simply a coincidence. We were riding in the car, my husband driving, Lucy on my lap. The only two places Lucy is ever truly relaxed is our bed, or our laps.

"Anyway, I started singing 'Indian Love Call,' and when I hit the first high note, my solo became a duet. It took her about thirty seconds to warm up her vocal cords, and then she was in full form. We sang on, blending our voices while the breeze carried our serenade out the windows and over the New Jersey treetops.

How to Bring Out Your Dog's Hidden Howl

Many dogs have howls hidden inside them and you can bring them out! Howling is a hoot for kids too. Some wolf sanctuaries even hold "Howl Nights," charging admission to people who wish to bay at the moon and howl along with the wolves. Sesame Street even created a video called *Sing, Hoot & Howl with the Sesame Street Animals* (*www.sesameworkshop.org/newshop*).

LindeTree music (*www.lindetree.nl*) is a Dutch company that offers nature sounds that not only soothe during thunderstorms, but can pique dogs' interest and help them howl. "Spirit of Africa" (which features real lions roaring) and "Land of the Loon" (featuring lake birds who offer their haunting and, to dogs, mysterious cries) seem to work well.

"Now, after almost three years living with Lucy, we have often 'asked' her to sing for us and others. All we need do is warble a high note and in a few seconds Lucy chimes in. Her head tilts upward and she vocalizes to the sky.

"But we'd love her even if she couldn't carry a tune!"

There's only a 2 percent difference between the domestic dog's DNA and that of the gray wolf, and wolves are arguably the best howlers in the world. A study of the "why" of howling and the complexity of howls shows that howling is both a natural science and a strategic matter.

For example, howling gives the howler's location away, which can be useful if a pack member is lost or harmful if a rival pack is nearby. Howling can be amplified or distorted by the terrain, so that those hearing the howls imagine a mighty pack where none exists. Wolves fooled General Ulysses S. Grant that way. He thought he was "at risk" from twenty wolves or more when it turned out he was listening to only a pair. There's even a name for this phenomenon. It is called the "beau geste" ("beautiful gesture") effect.

You can use wolf howls to inspire your dogs to sing. I recommend Judy Klein's CD, called *The Wolves of Bay Mountain*, a twenty-one-minute mix of all sorts of howls recorded in the mountains of east Tennessee at various times of the year. The wolves, who are known and named, give their winter chorus and even their mating calls. This should get your dog's ears to stand up (available at *www.wolfphotography.com*).

To learn more, the TV program *NOVA* has "howl-o-grams" on its Web site and recordings of all sorts of different howls, from the "lonesome" howl and the "pup" howl to the "confrontation" howl and the "mourning" howl (a solitary cry in which other wolves do not join). But the one we are looking for here is the "chorus" howl, in which everyone can throw back their heads and participate. So, check out *www.pbs.org/wgbh/nova/wolves/howl.html* if you would like to get some practice.

If you play an instrument (or even—especially!—if you don't), certain music can trigger howling. Californian Brandi Vallodolid tells me that her wonderful old mixed-breed dog, Milli, starts howling the moment her (most likely soon-to-be-ex) roommate, Stephanie, starts playing her trumpet. Other "dog people" report the same effect with kazoos, pianos, violins, trombones, flutes, and pipes of any kind. Some dogs "sing" to opera or to the blues. A child wrote in to the BBC's Web site to say that her dog, Lydia, can't resist singing along to Gerri Halliwell's "It's Raining Men." Another child writes that her dog *loves* Atomic Kitten! There's no accounting for taste.

So for your dog party, break out the band or splurge for a wind instrument, even a child's toy instrument; or buy a recording of howls or police and fire engine sirens; or get free downloads of both from *www.audiosparx.com* and *www.freesoundeffects.com*.

You can also do what wildlife biologist Stephanie Boyles does. Knowing that her dog, Sierra, loves howling to sirens, Stephanie tapes the TV show *Cops* just to give Sierra something to howl along to when she seems bored.

And if you are howling around a campsite or out in a meadow at night, you may wish to bring along the Dog Lighthouse, a rubber toy that lights up when your dog starts chewing it (*www.tail-waggers.com*). It's for you, not her, just in case you need to find your way in the dark.

Once you get into howling, you'll probably agree that it, more than anything else, provides the kind of "release therapy" participants get from a good cry—but without the handkerchief.

Bird Songs

Are your dogs bored? Let them have a party when you're at work by playing birdsong CDs to entertain and amuse them. I recommend *The Stokes Field Guide to Bird Song,* which offers 374 different birdcalls from the eastern United States (*www.amazon.com*) or *The Bird Song Ear Training Guide* (*www.birdwatching.com*). These CDs give each bird song and then announce the name of the bird you've just heard so they can help teach your dog English too!

The Car Party

Dog people have asked why there are cars named after the jaguar, the mustang, the colt, the stingray, and the rabbit, but none named for a dog when dogs, after all, are the only ones of the bunch who actually enjoy zipping about in one. Word has it that a petition is being circulated to get the Chrysler Eagle's successor to be christened the "Chrysler Beagle"—but I don't think your dog cares what the car's called, just that you open the door and say, "Want to go for a ride?"

Most dogs like nothing more than to ride in the car! As comedy writer Dave Barry says, "Dogs feel very strongly that they should always go with you in the car in case the need should arise for them to bark violently at nothing right in your ear."

Mikey Man, a middle-aged, twenty-five-pound terrier mix, lives with animal sanctuary owner Jill Bacchieri-Jones and is a rather typical dog when it comes to riding in the car. He starts off sitting in the back seat of the car but is so enchanted by traffic that whenever he sees that the car has started up the ramp to a freeway, no matter what freeway it is or how slowly or quickly Jill accelerates on the on-ramp, he insists on getting up in the front seat to have a better look.

Jill says she has occasionally tried to trick him by accelerating quickly on regular city streets and has even paralleled freeways, but he won't be fooled! His nickname is "the Freeway Man."

There are exceptions to a dog's love affair with the automobile. I know a very timid dog called Missy who gets the shakes just looking at a car (who knows what lies buried in her puppyhood?), and Joschi, a little mixed Pekingese who would probably prefer to go everywhere riding up a Chinese emperor's sleeve rather than in a car. Only you will know if a car party is right for your dog.

"She always knows exactly which car is a cab, and when one is coming to get us, she gets very excited as soon as she identifies it. She can tell the difference."

—Correspondent Heather Moore,
talking about her dog, Carly

The former president of the Washington Humane Society/ SPCA, Loretta Hirsh, has a theory that, to a dog, the car is a mobile den. What is more of a treat than to be with your people, secure in a private place (where you can take the fingers off any hand that dares to push through the window, even if that hand belongs to a park officer offering you an entrance ticket to a lovely green area), and it moves? The smells even come to you through the open window! It's like having someone else turn the pages of the newspaper as you relax with your loved ones.

The more fun trips in the car, the better, and a car party culminating in a picnic or a romp is the cat's meow, if you'll forgive the expression. A dog named Bubeleh knew she went for car rides for only two reasons: to go to "grandma's" house or to go to the vet, which, unfortunately, was fairly frequent due to recurring health problems.

Once in the car, she would sit apprehensively for the first mile. That was where one turn meant grandma and biscuits. The other way meant the dreaded V-E-T.

So, when the car turned to the right, the tail would start moving and excited yipping began and soon her whole body was wagging. The other turn elicited a crouched, quivering little body. How could she know when she was a good two miles from either destination, which way meant what? But dogs do, they do!

Her guardian tells of how, arriving at grandma's, Bubeleh once ran as fast as her little legs would carry her, dashing into the house, past her beloved grandma whom she loved and had not seen in almost two weeks. She started digging frantically at the couch where she had "buried" a chew stick twelve days earlier. Had she been thinking about it for days?

Many dogs are equally sensitive—some would say almost psychic—on the road home. Somehow, they know when the car is nearing its destination. They stand up, move around, bark, and so forth.

Travel Gear for Dogs

The Kyjen Company makes all sorts of travel gear for dogs, including car booster seats, travel bowls, suitcases, and a car bed pack that hooks into ordinary car seat belts. Visit *www.kyjen.com* for information about the products and where to purchase them.

A Cautionary Word

Don't ever forget that if it is warm and you have a dog in the car, even a quick stop can turn dangerous. Many's the person who has gone into the store "for a moment," only to be distracted by a friend, a cell phone call, or things on sale, not realizing that the temperature in the car is climbing to a dangerous or even fatal point. Even when the temperature is just about 70°F outside, the inside of a parked car can reach 120° to 175°F within minutes even with the windows cracked! Even in the shade, a car can quickly become an oven. Air conditioning can cut out, and heatstroke means brain damage. So stock up for the party *before* you leave home and put supplies in the car before you load the dogs so as to minimize your stops. And, if you do stop, be very vigilant in case it is too hot for Spot. Keep a travel bowl in the car at all times and be sure to bring fresh water.

Getting a Leg Up

Car too high and dog too short? There's always the Twistep, which assists in the loading and unloading of dogs into rear cargo spaces and attaches to the hitch of vehicles with high cargo floors. To find out where to buy one, visit *www.twistep.com*.

It goes without saying that no sensible, caring person would ever make their dog ride in the back of a pickup truck like an old sack of potatoes (it is illegal to do so in a growing number of states), given the danger of the dog catapulting from the truck bed should an accident occur, not to mention how hot a truck bed is on sensitive feet. And don't forget the doggy seatbelt!

It is also wise to carry a simple first-aid kit. This should contain a roll of bandages (so that you will not find yourself in the

predicament I did once on Vero Beach of having to use underpants as a tourniquet when Ms. Bea sliced open her pad); a bottle of Bach Rescue Remedy to calm traumatized nerves; a bottle of homeopathic arnica for pain; nail clippers; some Kwik Stop to staunch a bleeding nail; vet wrap bandages; and an emergency cookie. The arnica and Rescue Remedy are available at Whole Foods stores, most health stores, and from *www.bachflower .com*. Kwik Stop is available at *www.drsfostersmith.com*.

If you plan to let your dog get dirty (which he always appreciates), there are scads of car seat covers on the market, all washable, some elastic, some latch-ons, in every color and every model (see *www.orvis.com* or do a search on Google).

Okay. Get out the compass and the map, pack the car with all a dog and his pal needs, and, at the end of the ride, don't forget to play "Find the Bonio" or one of the other games in Chapter 7.

The Boat Party, or, A Doggie Would A-Boating Go

Some dogs have great sea legs. Santos the schipperke (Belgian barge dog) sailed aboard *Breath* from the Virgin Islands to Haiti to the Cape Verde Islands and the Azores. You can read about his adventures at *www.sailbreath.com* (click "History and Travels of BREATH"). The original Lassie saved the life of a sailor aboard the HMS *Formidable.* Portuguese water dogs are rumored to have sailed with the Spanish Armada.

Other dogs are like me: I have actually suffered from sea sickness while doing nothing more than bailing out a boat tied to a dock in a calm bayou. As a little girl, my dog Seanie and I were taken on long car rides to my grandmother's home in Bognor Regis (Regis indicates that the resort was favored by members of the royal family, who used to leave smoggy London to take in the sea air there). The mere *thought* of being near waves used to make Seanie and me race out of the car to throw up. Not very good going for two residents of a "proud, seafaring nation," and quite to the despair of my father who loved nothing more than to set off in a small boat during a thunderstorm!

Perhaps my own queasiness is why I am always upset to hear of adventurers who decide to sail the Atlantic in some small boat or the Pacific on a raft, taking along a dog or cat to ease their boredom. When lightning flashes, waves tower over and lash their tiny vessel, and things are touch-and-go out there, one can't help but pity the poor landlubber animals who, chances are, would not have said "Anchors aweigh!" if given a choice.

"Dogs are not our whole life, but they make our lives whole."

—*Author Roger Caras*

However, there are calm waters, stable craft, and sensible people who will not force a dog to do what a dog does not wish to do. And there are dogs who eagerly anticipate boarding a boat, waiting for their person to lower the ramp, buy a two-person kayak, and otherwise make room for a dog with sea legs.

Ms. Bea proved my jaded opinion of choppy waters did not float with her. She forced the issue one day by barking incessantly from the shore and then swimming out, her heavy body suddenly buoyant in the Annapolis Bay, to join my friend who was offshore in a fourteen-footer. (Ms. Bea, I may mention now that the statute of limitations has passed, was eventually busted for riding on a paddleboat in the Tidal Basin. The tourist attraction in question is a "no dogs allowed" reservoir next to the Jefferson Memorial in our nation's capital, but Ms. Bea jumped into a passing boat as a couple came paddling by too slowly to avoid her. U.S. Park Service officer be damned, Ms. Bea would not be budged.)

In San Francisco, there is a "Dog Day on the Bay" cruise, where for about $125 your dog (with you in tow) gets to sightsee at sea (well, bay) for two hours, feeling the spray on her face, feasting on a "doggie buffet," and even relieving herself, if she feels the urge, in a special sod-filled area called the "poop deck." This event benefits the San Francisco SPCA; visit *www .hornblower.com/dogday* for details.

Kayaking

Check with your local kayaking clubs too as many, like Water-Dog Outfitters in Hilton Head, South Carolina, allow dogs onboard. If you don't know how to kayak, it may be worth taking it up just for your dog's pleasure. Not whitewater kayaking, obviously.

Kayaking even has a paraplegic dog fan. Cooper is a dog who wears wheels to support his hind limbs but is at home in a tandem kayak. And Tibi is a kayaking dog who hangs out at Southwind

Kayak Center in Irvine, California, a company that gives invaluable instructions to beginners with dogs.

Among their tips: Choose a large, "family" or canoe-sized double kayak, preferably with the front seat removed, if your dog is medium to large. Have a towel handy to wrap a cold, wet pooch in. Use a life jacket with a handle on it to facilitate easy lifting of your dog in and out of the boat. For tips on kayaking with dogs, try *www.wonderpuppy.net,* Water-Dog Outfitters at *www.waterdogoutfitters.com,* and Southwind Kayak Center at *www.southwindkayaks.com.*

Dog Life Vests and Other Vital Accessories

Yes, as with all boaters, please be sure to look out for your dog's safety, too. Kit your dog out in a snazzy, heavy-duty life vest (available from *www.outdoorplay.com/headlines/dog_lifejackets.html, www.arcatapet.com,* and *www.altrec.com.* Fido Float Swim Aids with handles can be found at *www.funstufffordogs.com*). There are ones for all shapes and sizes. Dogs cannot beat a fast-moving current or keep afloat long enough without assistance in an emergency. Ramps are also available for wobbly dogs (see *www .petclassics.com*), and goggles (called "doggles") come with a comfy strap to keep water and UV rays out; they're available from *www.practicalsailingsolutions.com.* And remember to take their "high heels" off, meaning trim their nails, before they venture onto the yacht deck or into the kayak or dingy.

The "Take a Hike" Party

Dogs enjoy "getting away from it all" by going into the mountains, hills, or woods for a proper hike. Memories for both of you are made of such expeditions. You can make this party a movable feast too, if you like, by secreting little containers of Fib Ribs or Riblets (easy to eat and suitable for both humans and dogs; visit *www.gardenburger.com*) and other tasty mini-meals in your backpack. Every time you rest on a rock or by a stream you can break out a "course." Don't forget to bring lots of water for you and your dog. You can pick up a doggie back-pack, available in four different sizes from *www.dogdecor.com.* They are easy to remove and reattach during rest stops and include handy storage compartments so your dog can carry his own water supply (just make sure it's not too heavy!).

Dog sitter Leanne Siart, who is from the rugged West, has cherished photos of happy days backpacking in the Oregon Wilderness with Quinn, a vizsla mix, and her human friends. She says, "Quinn loved being on the trail, but what he loved even more was when we would come near a stream or pond. He would drink and drink until he was tanked up and then he'd drink more. We used to joke that Quinn was addicted to water.

"Come nightfall, our tent would be set up and sleeping bags rolled out. We'd crawl into our bags and Quinn would crawl in next to me. Quinn would crawl all the way down in the space below my feet. I have no idea how he breathed down there, but he wouldn't have it any other way. We would sleep all night like that and I was thankful for the extra body heat when the outside temperature dropped. Come morning, Quinn would somehow know the sun was up and push his way out and make his way to the stream for his long morning drink.

"Backpacking just wasn't the same once Quinn passed away. I miss him greatly."

So the lesson here is don't wait! Get out with your dog while you can and as often as you can. Time's a-wastin'.

First Aid and All That Jazz

I don't know about you, but my idea of camping is to stay at a Holiday Inn—nevertheless, do be sure your dog is up for anything truly vigorous before you get too adventurous and find yourself too far afield. In summer, heatstroke and exhaustion can occur in chubby, under-exercised, and old dogs, so be vigilant for the first signs of distress, for example, moving slowly, a bright red tongue, drooling, or hard panting. Do not push your dog to exceed her limits.

Pads that are not used to rough terrain or ice in winter may need protection to keep them from tearing and bleeding. Booties are available at *www.altrec.com* and similar sites, but don't wait to put them on when you need them, as some dogs will not tolerate booties out of vanity, because their feet are ticklish, or who knows!

For more safety tips, really sensible ones, take a quick look at *www .coyotecommunications.com/dogcamp.html* before adventuring.

Pop Up the Pup Tent

For your dog's comfort during hiking breaks or on camping trips (or afternoons just playing in the backyard), set up the Ultimate Dog Den, a super lightweight, easy to assemble, portable tent available from G. W. Little at *www.gwlittle.com*. Also check out the Mutt Hutt Tent made by Ruffwear. It pitches as easily as opening an umbrella and is available from *www.seniorpetproducts.com*. Finally, there's Pet Ego's Dog Bag, an igloo-style portable house that folds flat like those odd beach hats that convert into a Frisbee. It comes in four sizes and is available from *www.dog-bag.com*.

Après Hike Inspections

When you emerge from any ramble through the woods or in tall grass, immediately check your dog carefully for hitchhiking insect life. You do not want to find that your dog is taking a bad case of the itchy-scratchies home with him or has caught Rocky Mountain spotted fever or Lyme disease (do not panic—the risk of infection is extremely low, down in the low single digits even for those actually bitten by the "right" tick in an area where the disease is endemic—but infections do happen).

Use a fine-toothed flea comb on his coat and peer into ears and between toes for little ticks ("seed" ticks) who may be hiding there, happy to have found a home where they can start a (large) family.

The examination should be pleasant and disguised as a massage (see "The Total Relaxation Party" section later in this chapter, page 136).

Hiking Sites and Tips

For excellent pointers on dog-friendly hiking and beach sites, visit *www.hikewithyourdog.com*. Look for the article "What Beach?" Another good site to visit is *www.k9trailblazers.org*. This has information all about park hikes, even into some areas ordinarily off limits to dogs.

Let It Snow!

The Inuit may have a zillion names for snow, but, for many dogs—particularly the hardier cold-weather breeds and breed mixes like huskies, malamutes, malamutts (malamute-type mixes), Saint Bernards, and Newfies—snow, all snow, is summed up in one word: heaven! What's more, dogs aren't picky. They don't care what kind of snow it is. They'll take any snow you can throw (gently) at them. And, if the snow won't come to the malamute, you might take the malamute to the snow—if there's any within driving distance of where you and your dog hang your hats.

Dogs find snow beguiling, mystifying, and magical. When the door opens on a winter's day and a dog's nose twitches as it meets up with the crisp fresh air that means snow, and his eyes come alive as he sees the world has turned white, you can bet his heart is filled with joy. If it's raining, *fuhgeddaboudit*; but if it's snowing, *lemme at it*!

From all indications, a dog must find jumping about in the snow as refreshing as the feeling a polar bear gets when he slips into an icy pool on a sunny day. Most dogs instantly bury their snouts into piles of the stuff and emerge with blobs of snow all around their noses, looking a bit like police officers caught eating sugary doughnuts. Even small dogs have an Arctic blast!

Dogs don't need snowboards, skis, or sleds, but you may wish to slip some booties on their feet, especially if there is a danger of ice getting caught between their toes, a painful condition and a potentially dangerous one. Booties are also great protectors if those spoilsport snowplows are out sprinkling salt about, because that can burn a dog's feet. Here are some good places to find regular booties, snow and climbing booties, high-performance booties, and even ones for dogs who have arthritis (and leg wraps for them, too) but still want to frolic about in the snow as if they were mere pups: *www.wildmountainonline.com*, *www.handsnpaws.com*, and *www.seniorpetproducts.com*.

Lose your inhibitions, go slide down a hill on your bottom, and roll in the snow with your dog!

A Night at the Movies

Rin Tin Tin was the very first dog star in Hollywood, with at least twenty-two movies to his credit. The next most famous dog movie stars are Lassie and little Toto from *The Wizard of Oz*. And, just as it is the rule that women's magazines sell more if they feature women on their covers, dogs "buy"—or at least like to watch—movies starring not, as you might think, cats and squirrels, but . . . other dogs.

According to *Washingtonian* magazine, 39 percent of readers report that their dogs watch TV. If you love television, you may be just the right couch companion for your dog's movie "night in." You'll be in good company, as a glance at the testimonials on the dog movie Web sites illustrate, with rave reviews by everyone from nuclear physicists to whole families, from grannies to tots.

Let's Have a Dog Party!

"He is scared to death of firecrackers so every Fourth of July we close the blinds and have a movie party."

—Writer Angela Malcom, talking about her dog, Ralph

At the top of the list of movies for your dog is one cunningly entitled *The Movie for Dogs* (*www.themoviefordogs.com*). The movie features dogs jumping into water, dogs barking and playing in the park, and dogs competing in games, as well as a wealth of sounds to accompany the action, including a doorbell, door knocker, whistles, and bird songs. If your dog is lonely when you are out, as she surely is, this movie is perfect. You don't have to be home for your dog to watch it. It is G rated.

Other DVDs to send away for include *Pooch TV* at *www.poochtv.com*, which sells for under $10, or *Dogs Do TV!*, a one-hour DVD of action-packed video fun for dogs (free to anyone who purchases a CD from *www.justdogsrecords.com*). And if you want to watch something together, try *Lady and the Tramp*. It's not only a great message movie and a love story, but it has lovely barking in it.

Top Tip

When you've popped the corn, try nutritional yeast as a topping for your dog. Don't salt her share.

Let's Have a Luau!

Aloha! There's something to be said about a state that helps simplify your relationships by having the same word for "hello" and "goodbye" and that has hills and beaches that any *nani* (beautiful) and *akamai* (smart) dog would love to run on.

There's also something to be said for a state that knows how to throw one of the most colorful parties imaginable, the luau. A proper luau lasts four days! Unless you own some tens of thousands of acres of land and know an awful lot of people, you'll never be able to compete with the one King Kamehameha put on in 1847—there were 10,000 guests and enough underground fires to rival Krakatoa. But your backyard luau can still be terrific fun for dogs as well as adult humans and their infants.

If you have an enthusiastic water dog who isn't afraid of the ocean, you can hold your luau at the beach and teach him to surf, although that does not mean dragging him into the waves.

Dress Up Island-Style

While it is perfectly acceptable for dogs to appear at a luau in the nude (as lots of people do when bathing at Waikiki at dawn) or to wear a simple, hibiscus-patterned bandana, humans may decide to go native. For men, that can mean going bare-chested or wearing a floral shirt or a sarong.

For women, nothing can be easier than slipping on a moo-moo (basically, a smock, under which you can wear trousers, shorts, or whatever you like), a cloth wrap, or a grass skirt and a flower in your hair. Mock grass skirts are available from the

Oriental Trading Company and come in all colors. And don't forget the leis, those wonderful flower necklaces, now available in plastic, of course. Each arriving guest should be garlanded and told "Aloha."

You can dress up the table with an artificial grass skirt from the Oriental Trading Company (anyone caught putting the skirt on the dog should be sent home without supper), which sells a whole Hawaiian theme party pack, including plastic leis, pineapple and coconut plastic cups, drink parasols and hibiscus flower drinking straws, a pineapple piñata for kids, and the ever-popular hula hoop (*www.orientaltrading.com*). Lest you think we're focusing too much on you and have forgotten your four-footed friend, the luau has special treats she will adore.

Make a Pooch Poi

Poi is perhaps Hawaii's most well-known native dish, not a pie but a pudding. It is a paste made from pounding taro root with a pestle, and it used to be given to people to stop them from feuding, a sort of "peace poi" if you will.

Poi is a bit of an acquired taste for humans, like Marmite. If you find yourself short of fresh taro root (and who isn't?), you can make a look-alike version that your guests and dogs may find palatable:

All you do is make Cream of Wheat and then stir in peanut butter, or any other flavor your dog enjoys, for his pleasure and that of other dog guests; substitute pineapple chunks for your human guests.

Hawaiian Haupia for Hounds and Humans

Another traditional dish is haupia, an authentic Hawaiian pudding. Since most dogs love coconut (some guardians put coconut oil in their dog's chow for a shiny coat and other health benefits; visit www.coconutdiet.com *for more information), this goes down as a treat with most of them. The ancient recipes call for boiling real coconuts, but your dog doesn't have time to wait, so here's an easy version (humans may wish to add sugar or syrup to theirs):*

    4 cups coconut milk
  2½ cups water
    1 cup cornstarch

Put the coconut milk and water into a saucepan, boil, then simmer until foamy. Add cornstarch. Cook over low heat until it thickens and is smooth, meaning that the coconut milk fat has melted. Allow it to cool. Top with toasted coconut or eat it plain or, for humans, sweetened.

Learn to Wag Your Tail

The hula involves a lot of wiggling of your nether regions, something dogs do naturally and well. You dog will be fascinated to watch you try to master this maneuver.

There is a whole language of the hands that is guaranteed to interest your dog, and dogs often like to dance along—unless the music is too loud for their delicate ears, so choose ukulele music or other Hawaiian music and play it softly. There are lots of hula CDs and instruction manuals available.

Here's the basic hula step. Ham it up—your dog will love it:

Put your arms out, at chest height, and move them gracefully, with an up and down motion, as if imitating tiny waves on the shore. Keep your fingers together.

Move your arms slowly to the right, swaying to the music, then, with your knees slightly bent, take a short step to the right, slide your left foot up to join your right and repeat.

Go the other way, by moving both your arms to the left, taking a short step to the left, then sliding your right foot up to join your left, knees slightly bent as before.

You can now act out scenes with your hands as you move your hips and move to the right and left, putting your arms over your head, making a sun to one side, making birds flying away, or doing the cradle, and so on. For more hula how-tos try *Hula for Everyone* (which also teaches you hula songs, such as "The Hawaiian Wedding Song" and "Blue Hawaii") or one of the other hula DVDs available for $24.95 from *www.hawaiicity.com*.

Two Extra Treats for Your Dog

Since roasting a suckling pig is decidedly politically incorrect these days, and for good reason, give your dog and his dog guests a soy pigs' ear to chew on instead. From Wow-Bow Distributors, vegan "pigs' ears" are available at *www.petacatalog.com*.

And if your dog's sleeping spot needs a summer lift, you might visit *www.coolpetstuff.com* for a Hawaiian print bed that is perfect for an after-party nap.

Aloha!

Una Fiesta Mexicana

Since this party is so perfect for children, I've put it in that section of the book (see Chapter 9, page 142). But if you don't have kids, don't let that stop you. A Mexican Fiesta is great for your dog and your guests.

Oktoberfest

Your dog does not have to be German to enjoy this party, and neither do your guests. Thankfully, dogs are not nationalists. Oh, that we would follow their lead!

I lived for many years with a dachshund named Daisy who went everywhere with my family when we lived in India and who fretted mightily over the places my father took us: into the Little Rani of Kutch, for example, a desert with hard-to-detect patches of sinking sand into which you and your Jeep might sink and keep sinking, never to be seen again; and up into the Everlasting Snows of the Himalayas. If Yeti, the Abominable

Snowman, didn't get you in your tent, the wild bears just might. As a result, Daisy was constantly checking to make sure she hadn't lost a member of the family. She would run back and forth along perilous paths (once over an ice bridge in Kashmir) to make sure we were all accounted for.

Her previous guardians, long gone back to the Fatherland from this Indian outpost, were German, and so I imagine that the words running through her head as she located each individual family member, were *"ein, zwei, drei,"* and so on.

We never thought to see if Daisy had a penchant for sauerkraut, but most dogs do not, as pickled foods are not generally to their taste. I am sure, however, that all that counting parched her throat and that she would have loved a sip of beer on those days when, as Kipling reported, only Mad Dogs and Englishmen (my father, in this case) were out in the midday sun (see page 131 for nonalcoholic beer dogs can drink safely).

So, break out the trestle tables, buy some beer steins, put on the oom-pah-pah music, and let's have a party.

Was Ist Das *on Your Head?*

A hat with a plastic feather will allow you to pass yourself off as Tyrolean, but make sure the hat doesn't upset the dogs, as some hats do. Any shortish shorts with suspenders can serve as updated lederhosen as long you wear them with "sensible" shoes and long socks. A waistcoat (vest to you!) and a pipe or accordion around your neck will complete the outfit. Women who feel like exposing their cleavage under a puffy blouse and wearing embroidered skirts and white stockings can complete the picture by braiding their hair or wearing a fun wig with braids. Your dog has more dignity than all this but frankly doesn't care what you look like. But you'll now be in the right frame of mind for something she *will* care about: *watching you dance as foolishly as possible.*

The Jolly Dog and Other Polkas

According to *www.fezziwigs.org*, it's easy to do the Jolly Dog Polka. All you do is stop when the music stops, at which point you place your hands on your hips and sing a little song, like "Fa la la, fa la la" etc., stepping first to the right and then to the left. You then sing, "Slap, bang, clap, pat, what jolly dogs are we," and start all over again. Turn and change partners, continue to polka down the line.

Get it? Got it? Good!

Veggiefurters for All

Let's face it: Fried cabbage, onion pie, and German chocolate cake are not for dogs. My suggestion is to fry the onions separately for the human guests and put some Yves or other tasty soy wieners and veggie burgers on the grill (*www.yvesveggie.com*). That way every Herr and Hund can eat to their fill without taking in enough lard and other animal fats to sink the *Bismarck*.

Dog-Themed Beer

You can also perk up the party with just the right beer. Try Flying Dog Brewery's "Flying Dog," "Road Dog," and "Tire Bite," which have Hunter S. Thompson–esque drawings on the labels (*www.flyingdogales.com*).

Among other suitable (and good) beers are Spanish Peaks ("No Whiners"), Old Brown Dog (named after a dearly loved dog named Olive), and Pete's Wicked Ale. Pete Slosberg, the brewery founder, credits his dog Millie for being his muse and becoming the brewery's mascot. Spuds McKenzie was a Johnny-come-lately!

There is also, believe it or not, "beer" brewed just for dogs, and dogs apparently love it. And it's nonalcoholic because, ask yourself, who wants a drunk dog in the house? Talk about "hair of the dog"!

The company that makes beer for dogs did so because the owners like pleasing their own adopted dog, Kodi. The story, as they tell it, began in the summer of 2002 when they took Kodi camping.

"While sitting around the campfire at night, we noticed that if we put our beers down on the ground next to our chairs, he'd knock them over and try to lick it from the dirt!" And that is how they discovered Kodi's "affinity for beer."

So, the folks at Dog Star Brewing Company in Northern California now make Happy Tail Ale just for Kodi and any of his friends who can get their paws on it. It's made with malted barley and vitamins, and it's nonalcoholic, of course, because dogs make their own fun. For ordering details and to read more about dogs and beer, go to the aptly named site *www.beerfor dogs.com*!

Not that beer gets served in a cocktail glass, but so as to prove the market caters to just about anything doggie, there is now a "swank cocktail set" for dogs who have had a "ruff day." It will set you back $65 and consists of a "Mutt-ini" dog bowl, a "Cosmo-paw-litan" dog bowl, both fashioned like cocktail glasses, and a chew toy garnish in each glass. Visit *www.muttropolis.com.*

And what's the perfect present for your Oktoberfest? Why, a chew-toy VW bug, of course.

Prost!

A Reunion Party: Down Memory Lane

"We had a party for our six-year-old Italian greyhound. He got gingerbread cookies and we played a video of a greyhound reunion. When he heard his friends barking, he ran over to the TV and sat there. We love him dearly."

—Greyhound rescuer Jeanne Beaulieu,
talking about Max

A reunion takes many forms and can involve one long lost friend or relative, one separated litter, or, in the case of the Greyhound Companions of New Mexico (*www.gcnm.org*), a group that rescues and re-homes greyhounds—140 long-lost chums! It's hard not to be bowled over by the idea of that many ex-track greyhounds cavorting about in one place like a herd of rather delicate bison, but that's how many people get excited enough to show up with their dogs.

Judy Paulsen is the founder of Greyhound Companions of New Mexico. Ask her about their events and she is off like a racing dog out of a starting gate.

Says Judy, "Suki relished this reunion; her joy was something to see. She had been confiscated from a man who had got his hands on some ex-track dogs and was breeding them to hunt and kill rabbits." (If you are surprised to hear of such treatment, a look inside the world of dog racing is enough to turn your stomach. Treated as nothing more than "running machines," most greyhounds live in cages and are kept muzzled by their trainers at all times.)

"She had been quite sick when we took her and her littermate into our adoption program," says Judy, "but after lots of TLC and vet care, she recovered and became a happy, healthy girl. Now she feels that the world should revolve around her, and rightfully so after all she's been through!"

Suki is also a most mischievous greyhound.

"So far," Judy reports, "she has destroyed two couches, three remote controls, and numerous wardrobe items and chewed almost all the way through a wall! All this happened while her people were at home with her! All it takes is for a back to be turned briefly and Suki sees this as an invitation to search and destroy."

As for the big reunion, here's how Judy described it: "One hundred and forty-one dogs in one park, almost all beyond excited to see familiar friends with long noses. All the dogs had a day to remember, but Suki behaved like the guest of honor, scampering about nosing every dog and human at the park."

Judy's last remark surprised me: "The greyhounds don't run and run and run at the reunion. They take their retirement very seriously, and running is no longer as important to them since they don't have to do it to stay alive. They just hang out!"

Where did your dog come from? Forget tracing your genealogy back to the *Mayflower*. Who cares? What's important here is your dog's recent history. Does she have brothers and sisters, even a mother, somewhere, who would drop their bones and come running, almost bursting with happiness, were they to see her again? Or did she come from a foster home or a dog "orphanage," where your inquiry might reveal that she was waiting all those months for you to come along, not alone but in the company of some dog pal in a similar predicament? If you've seen your dog staring wistfully at the mailbox, could it be that she wasn't hoping to take a bite out of the mail carrier, but was hoping for a postcard?

When I visited the Mayhew Trust Dogs Home, on the outskirts of London, last year, I found two odd-looking mixed terriers, standing on top of a bench in their run, barking their heads off at thin air. It seemed they had lived together for years in one room of a house. They were both neurotic as can be from never having set one paw outside, not even into the hallway. Thankfully, they were attractive dogs—more attractive if you were hard of hearing—so both were quickly spoken for. Unfortunately, they were to be in new homes miles apart from each other, unable to rub noses except in their dreams. I asked the director if it would be possible to reunite them for walks once in a while, just for comfort's sake. "That's a good idea," she said and scribbled a note on their cage card. I hope they met up again.

At least with your dog, you are in complete control. You can make such reunions a reality!

After you answer, "Where did my dog come from?" the next thing to do is to sit down and make a list of all the dogs your dog has ever known. Who has moved away, and can you find them? Has someone in the neighborhood drifted off to a different dog park or started taking their walks at a time when you and yours are not out and about? What about old pals from obedience school or doggy daycare? Some sleuthing and deep thought may help you create a "pack" for your dog that will make the number of tourists on the National Mall in August look like child's play.

That's how to get started. To end your reunion (although one hopes it will be one of many), sing to your dog from the Scottish bard Robert Burns's "Auld Lang Syne." You know the tune. For lyrics, which certainly have meaning for anyone who's ever had a dog companion, and the meaning of the old Scottish words, see *www.hogmanay.net*.

The Total Relaxation Party

Who doesn't want to relax? Who doesn't have tired muscles? Well, if you do, you spoiled person, your dog needs it in spades.

Why do dogs deserve relaxation more than most of us? Well, not only because they don't get to play with executive stress balls during the working day. Think of it: Most of them have total responsibility for guarding the house from all sorts of nogoodniks, like the postal carrier who is trying to deliver bills you don't want; the yard from (the horror of it!) *cats and squirrels*; the *refrigerator*, for goodness' sake; the beds; the *food bowls* (can you imagine!); not to mention you and anyone else in your family.

A dog, even one who weighs in at a few pounds, knows full well that she is Knight Errant and Protector for the whole damned lot since you are apparently unable to bring in more help. She knows intuitively that there'll be hell to pay if she allows some UPS interloper to put a package on the doorstep without being severely warned about her teeth.

This kind of nonstop vigilance has to be exhausting.

Dorothea Tanning wrote this poem that was published in the *New Yorker* that conjures up just the right image of the stresses dogs experience. This one takes place on moving day.

"Wisdom Tinged with Joy"
Out of the mouths of city dogs
Have come some useful truths.
Barks and whines—noise to some—
Are fraught with ancient wisdom.
A dog, to share his basic instinct,
Will warn, say, of the landlord
At the door to spoil your day.
"Don't open," he barks. In vain.
When the van is loaded: laptop,
Mattresses, and microwave,
A wise dog rides in stoic silence
To the new (smaller apartment)
Where joyously he soon resumes
His job of watching over rooms.

Add to this constant sense of duty how tense your dog must get trying to figure out if you are only jangling your car keys because you are absent-mindedly using them as percussion instruments or if you are planning on getting in the auto and driving away. Away? And, she wonders, are you on the phone to a friend or are you making an appointment for her shots? Is it that you feel more comfortable in your track shoes this evening or are you about to go off for a run? And if you are off for a run, will you be taking her or not? If not, will you be late for dinner or will everyone get fed on time?

It's tiring just *thinking* about what a dog must be thinking. We don't speak their language; they work hard trying to figure us out.

If you have concluded from these small examples that it is indeed a miracle that your dog is not on Prozac (and forgive me if she is, but perhaps the root cause of her problems may be stress that needs to be addressed), a massage may be the very gift your dog would enjoy most. And dog massages come with at least two bonuses: They usually end up being great therapy for you, too, and they allow you to conduct stealthy physical exams that may reveal, early in the game, any nasty little growths or other problems your dog might have acquired.

Your touch is something your dog longs for. For some dogs, even being groomed is a bigger treat than getting a new toy. Stroking your dog's coat and patting her lightly is a soothing and reassuring experience that should not be reserved for when she is recovering from surgery. A light touch is the key.

Some Basics of How to Massage Your Dog

The best massage would probably be given with your teeth, as that is how dogs massage their own skin. Dexter is a dog who likes to massage his pals, Rowdy and Sunny, by running his teeth over their heads and paws as if he is chewing corn on the cob. He nibbles at them, stimulating every nerve as he works methodically. His person says it "paralyzes them with pleasure."

PETA member Patti Tillotson's dog, a shepherd/Akita mix named Maguire, loved a guinea pig called Mabel and very much enjoyed letting Mabel give him a massage by chewing the whole length of his tail! And writer Kathy Guillermo reports that Josie, her Jack Russell terrier mix, is apparently interested in massage, too, but as the giver, not the recipient. When Kathy's grooming her cat, Josie comes over and nibbles the cat's fur in an apparent attempt to help.

Happily, you do not have to use your teeth. Nor do you need to be a professional dog masseur to do a bang-up job of massage, although you can always turn to a professional. More and more spas for dogs are springing up (search on the Web under "dog massage" and your city's name), some offering Reiki and acupuncture too. But just be calm and relaxed yourself, slow down, and follow these simple rules:

Some people use massage oil on smooth-coated dogs, but I find it messy. Your touch alone is sufficient to transport her to a state of bliss.

First, make sure your dog is properly exercised so she isn't thinking of "walkies" while you work her muscles. Make sure, too, that she is in a restful mood. I heard a comedian once joke that she is such a wound-up type-A personality that she has to drink a cup of espresso before she meditates. A pent-up dog who hasn't had a good walk or run today is not going to sit still for, and won't fully benefit from, the massage. It will be like trying to get a bee to sit still when the queen is on the move.

Second, remove all distractions, like small children and other animals.

Third, put on some soothing music at a low level, lower than you might normally play it (see Chapter 12 for pointers).

Now, gently start petting your dog, running your fingertips, just the fingertips—first two fingertips, then four—over her shoulders. Progress down her back, going with the grain of her coat. When you get to her tail, if she is relaxed, imagine drawing all the pent-up energy that you have pulled along with your fingers out of her tail, all the way to the very tip and into the air and beyond.

If that went over well, you can return to the shoulders and knead them a bit, ending up, as with a human massage, by pushing down a bit with the palm of your hand and perhaps even drumming on the shoulders.

Go back to the shoulders and ever so gently caress her face, running your hands over her eyes and down her cheeks and muzzle. Move down under her chin, a favorite "zone out" massage point, and rub her chest with your thumbs or the palm of your hand (unless she is very tiny, in which case two fingers will do the trick).

Find your dog's temples and softly caress her there by using small circular movements with your fingers. Gently work the stress out of her ears one at a time and then rub behind her ears just for fun.

I like to leave the legs, and especially the toes, until last because, although they may need the massage most, they are also likely to be the most ticklish or sensitive part of your dog's body. Memories of having her nails clipped may make her want to kick or not allow her to lie very still, and she may not tolerate someone rubbing her legs, even quite lightly. It depends on how relaxed she is and on her life experiences. Be extra careful if your dog has any joint problems at the knees or elbows or any hip socket distress (hip dysplasia).

For extra credit, you can run your fingers inside your dog's mouth and massage her gums. If she is sufficiently zombielike at this stage, this exercise also allows you to look for dental problems and to determine if it is time to have her teeth cleaned. Be crafty about sneaking in these medical exams or she will cotton on and opt out!

If you only massage your dog for a few minutes, you will have done a good deed. If you can do a full workup, your dog will be on cloud nine. If you'd rather not use your bare hands, try the Groom-a-Pet Massage Mitt, which fits hands of all sizes. It is available in many pet supply stores and from *www.shop.com* and other online supply shops for about $8.

Try to do a little massage once a day or several times a week, and you will have the most laid-back, grateful dog on the block. Before you know it, your dog will be using your credit card to buy a whirlpool bath and a yoga mat. See Resources for wonderful books offering further massage instruction.

9

Getting KIDS in on the Act

"He loved children with ice cream cones in their hands and would try everything to steal the cone from them. No child with an ice cream was spared. He would just go up ever so quietly, look for the right moment and gently take the ice cream out of the child's hand."

—*Schoolteacher Andrea Müller, describing her dog, Tobi*

Kids and dogs are a natural match. Not only do they both love ice cream, they usually don't have pretensions either. They both love to run and jump and make noise, and getting dirty is considered nothing to make a fuss about.

Every sociologist and child psychologist knows that bonding with a dog in childhood is a mystical and helpful experience that has its rewards in a lifetime appreciation of other people who do not look, talk, or have interests identical to one's own.

Back in the 1800s, George T. Angell founded the Massachusetts Society for the Prevention of Cruelty to Animals (MSPCA). In addition to stepping out into the street to stop horses from pulling wagons overloaded with bricks and reprimanding the men who whipped their nags up the cobbled streets, Mr. Angell taught kindness to animals. He could often be found in "poor schools," teaching children the importance of empathy.

Kindness to "beasts" was a relatively new and seemingly bourgeois consideration to many, and Mr. Angell was dressed down on more than one occasion for his "frivolous" lessons to the poor when there were "more serious" social issues to address. Mr. Angell was undeterred. He reminded his detractors that out of these schools would come the murderers and muggers of tomorrow, but that by teaching them to put themselves in the place of those they did not immediately relate to, he was "working at the roots." To teach a child to be kind to a caterpillar, he said, does as much for the child as for the caterpillar.

So, by all means, include children in your dog party. It's good for both.

The Importance of Introducing Strange Kids to Strange Dogs

Before kids meet a new dog, and vice versa, it is wise to explain to the children that dogs can be scared by them and the noises they make. Tell the children that proper introductions are a must and that there are a few "do's" and "don'ts" when playing with and near dogs.

1. Never run up to a dog you don't know. A dog may think you are attacking him! See how dogs greet each other. The new dog usually stands still and lets the other or bigger dog sniff him. Let the dog sniff you first. (Offer your hand rather than patting him on the head.) That's their way of saying, "Hi, my name is. . . ."

2. If you are screaming or yelling, dogs may run up, thinking you are attacking another child and need to be bitten so that you will stop. If you see excited dogs coming toward you, stop making noise and stand still. Do not wave your arms; keep your arms by your side and let everything calm down. Do not look the dog in the eye, because that is how, in the wild, dogs challenge each other. Look at his paws!

3. Do not make sudden movements near a dog; you may spook him and he may feel he has to defend himself.

4. Don't run away or scream if a dog approaches you in an unfriendly way. Stand still and be very quiet. If he jumps on you, curl into a ball.

You do need to make sure that kids don't drive the dog(s) crazy or vice versa! The key to including children is not to forget that this is *your dog's* special day. Obviously no tail pulling, eye poking, or other bullying is ever allowed, and children can be gently instructed in the importance of *letting the dog win* some of the games. After all, it would be no fun for the guest of honor if a human being, a child at that, *always* gets to the ball first and *always* wins the tug of war!

To engage your child, there are lots of party Web sites for birthday parties and the like that offer dog-themed paper plates and cups, little dog tag take-home mementos, paper party hats with happy dogs on them, and even wash-off dog tattoos. Dog ears and dog noses are also a big hit and are easy to get your paws on. For dog-themed party supplies, see *www.prettypartyplace .com, www.partycity.com, www.birthdayzbyshindigz.com,* or *www.birthdayexpress.com.*

Here are some excellent ways to help kids give the dog(s) a rest and have a terrific time at your dog's party.

A Mexican Fiesta

Ay, Chihuahua! Whether you have one of these itty-bitty dogs or not, you are permitted to throw a party honoring the birthplace of one of the dearest tiny beings in the world and all her cousins! You can also invite cats as honorary Chihuahuas.

Kids love a Mexican-themed party because they can dress up in sombreros and gaucho pants or flouncy Spanish skirts and lace mantillas. You can put Latin music on the CD player—which means that someone can teach them (or *they* can teach *you*) how to dance the Macarena, the cha-cha, the rumba, the salsa, and the merengue. Most dogs love to dance, so to speak, and if there are lots of dogs, lots of dog paws will be on lots of shoulders and around kids' waists with little encouragement (just make sure the dogs are indeed *willing* partners). Latin-themed parties are also a hit because the food can be great kid stuff. Kids enjoy eating tacos. I recommend filling them with soy sausage crumbles, which are good for kids and which they love getting all over their faces. If you're not picky, the dogs can lick it off them. (And if you *are* picky, remember: Dog saliva is far less likely to spread disease than the saliva of a child.)

The Music

There are lots of Latin dance music CDs to choose from, including *The Ultimate Latin Album 7* and *El Nuevo Cha Cha Cha* from *www.danceshopper.com*. Also, check out *www.napster.com*. For Latin dance moves, check out www.ballroomdancers.com/dancers.

Making a Piñata

They may lick your face, but don't let dogs lick the glue if the kids are going to make their own piñatas (piñata-creating should also be done at a pre-party at least two days earlier so the glue has time to dry properly). There are lots of different piñata "recipes" on the Web but here's one to get you started:

Round up:

2 cups flour

3 cups water

1 10-inch balloon

  Newspaper, cut into long 1-inch-thick strips

  Paint, crayons, or markers

  Colored crêpe paper

  Glue

  String

  Toys and candy to put inside

Instructions:

1. Blow up the balloon and tie the end. Mix the flour and water together until it makes a smooth, but not too runny, paste. Dip the newspaper strips, one at a time, into the flour/water mixture and squeeze off any extra. Carefully place the strips on the balloon until it is covered, but leave a hole at the top. Smooth over all crinkles and air bubbles. Set aside and let dry a few hours. Add another layer of

newspaper strips dipped in the mixture over the balloon and let dry. Repeat with one more layer, making sure you leave the hole at the top. When dry, pop and remove the balloon.

2. Decorate your piñata with different designs and colors. If desired, hang colored crêpe paper from the sides and bottom with glue. To add anything to your basic piñata structure, such as points of a star, paint cardboard or use thick colored paper filled with scrunched up newspaper, and glue or tape your additions right onto your base. I don't like the idea of beating an animal, even a papier-mâché one, so I'd suggest making the piñata in the shape of some-*thing* rather than some*one*. Punch two small holes in the top near the opening and thread a large piece of string through the two holes.

3. Fill your piñata (through the hole you left at the top) with candy, toys, dog treats, or any other fun surprises. You should also fill it with strips of newspaper so the surprises are not all in one clump.

4. Hang your piñata in the air with the string, and have fun!

The process is messy, so cover the floor. And, when the moment comes when kids would normally bash the piñata, try a less scary (to dogs) and dangerous (to all) technique. Put the piñata on the ground and each child can make one tear in the "body" of the piñata with their hands. The dogs can join in! (Do be sure the dogs do not get the candy or pieces of crêpe paper.)

You can also buy a ready-made piñata from party stores or online, and there are even places where you can order a custom-made piñata. Visit *www.orientaltrading.com* or *www.pretty partyplace.com*.

The Chihuahuas

As for Chihuahuas, who have to spend most of their time clambering onto couches to be at eye level with you, they were first mentioned in a letter from Christopher Columbus to the King of Spain, describing the wonders in the New World.

Chihuahuas are believed to have lived all over South America, and archaeologists have found etchings of this little dog from back in the Toltec times of the ninth century. Later, the Olmec tribes, who called Chihuahuas "Techichi," ate them! I've heard a Chihuahua guardian say of her cute little dog, "He's *so* adorable, I could eat him right up."

Christopher Columbus thought that Chihuahuas were mute, but he must have had a cornhusk in his ear. My Conchita, like most Chis of my acquaintance, made up for any "deficiency" in her size with her big voice. A gas station attendant who made the mistake of touching the windshield with a squeegee ten years ago probably still has ringing in his ears.

Putting on the Dog

To let the kids' creativity shine, you might give each young human a white T-shirt and a palette of fast-drying acrylic paints.

Hold a contest (letting everyone win) for the best dog drawing made on the shirt, or just let them paint away. Of course, provide aprons or encourage the children to be outfitted in clothes where a few dabs of paint won't matter. Warn parents that the child who arrives looking like a pristine angel may not return home in the same condition. Everyone can model their shirts afterward and tell stories about the dog they have chosen to paint. Oh, and make sure the dogs stay out of the paint!

Dog Joke, Riddle, and Caption Contests

As with all kids' and dogs' contests, everyone's a winner of course. Kids can remember jokes, puns, and other silly dog patter or make it up as they go along. Have no fear, kids find everything funny. Here are a few puns and jokes to break the ice and get them guessing and giggling:

Q. Why do dogs wag their tails?
A. Because no one else will do it for them!

Q. What do you get if you cross a sheepdog with a rose?
A. A collie-flower!

Q. Why do dogs bury bones in the ground?
A. Because you can't bury them in trees, can you?

Q. What's almost as clever as a dog who can tell time?
A. A spelling bee!

Q. If English humans say "toodle-oo" to mean "goodbye," what do English dogs say?

A. "Poodle-oo!"

The last two riddles were submitted by Lee, a little boy in Texas, and Katie, age seven, of West Sussex, England, to a fabulous interactive Web site for kids called *www.loveyourdog.com*. Among other helpful bits there, you'll find book recommendations and lessons in kindness. Want to bring a lesson like this into your party?

Other amusements include having the children guess and shout out the punchlines to existing jokes or jokes you make up. Here are two easy-as-pie ones to start them off with:

What do you call a dog in summer? "A hot dog!"
And what do you call a dog in winter? "A chilly dog!"

Another cute game is the "Mutt Game." (By the way, we shall have no snobbery! So-called purebreds are mutts, too. Did you know that? They are just mixtures of dogs, bred together by humans looking to satisfy their own desires for a dog with a big-barreled chest suitable for fighting, long legs for racing, and so on.) Some wag (no pun intended) came up with the following ways to create new dogs, thankfully in name only, by mixing the breeds. Children can guess the final result if you give them the breed mix, or you can have them make up their own "new breeds." Here are some examples to get you started.

What do you call:

Collie + Lhasa apso?
A *collapso*: a dog that folds up for easy transport.

Spitz + chow chow?
A *spitz-chow*: a dog that throws up a lot.

Irish water spaniel + English springer?
An *Irish springer*: a dog fresh and clean as a whistle.

Newfoundland + basset hound?
A *newfound asset hound*: a dog for financial advisers.

Terrier + bulldog?
A *terribull*: a dog that makes awful mistakes.

Bloodhound + Labrador?
A *blabador*: a dog that barks incessantly.

Collie + malamute?
A *commute*: a dog who travels to work.

You can also draw or cut out pictures of dogs in silly situations, give a copy to each child, and have them work on captions to go in the little balloon over the dog's head or below the artwork, in the style of the *New Yorker*'s own cartoon caption contest. It also works well to whiteout and then photocopy children's comics with dogs in them and have the children imagine what is happening and fill in the story frame by frame.

An Interactive Poem

Here's a poem called "Rags" (from *www.canteach.ca*) that kids can act out with their hands. Get them to repeat after you, and then do it until they have it memorized!

I have a dog his name is Rags
(*Put your hands on the sides of your head, fingers up, like ears*)

He eats so much his tummy sags
(*Make circles on your tummy with one hand*)

His ears flip flop and his tail wig-wags
(*Hands up to make ears, then "wag" your fingers on your rump*)

And when he walks, he walks zig-zag!
(*Walk three exaggerated sideways steps forward, right foot first*)

He goes flip-flop, wig-wag, zig-zag!
(*Hands on the ears, hands on the rump, walking forward as above*)

He goes flip-flop, wig-wag, zig-zag! (*Again*)

He goes flip-flop, wig-wag, zig-zag! (*Again*)

I love Rags and he loves me!
(*Turn around and blow a kiss, then start all over again in the direction you are now facing*)

10 *Planning the Canine*
PARTY MENU

"Bailey loves pizza. When the delivery folks come to the house I always put her in another room so there's no risk that she'll scare them, as she is very big and friendly, with a gigantic bark. All I have to do is tell her, 'the pizza man is coming' and she runs to that room and sits down to wait."

—*Patricia Trostle, humane educator,*
talking about her dog, Bailey

In England, there is the phrase "He made a dog's dinner of it," meaning that he made a big, fat mess. That perfectly illustrates the point that dogs, unlike fussy French chefs, couldn't give a hoot about presentation. If what's in their bowl looks like a Jackson Pollack painting come to life, they are happy. That's another big timesaver with a dog party!

However, because *you* may have different ideas (or you may *be* a fussy French chef), I won't leave out ideas for dishes or just plain grub that are not only tasty but tastefully plated and presented to get *you* and your guests in a party mood.

Although I have included dips and more for the human side of the menu, you will see that there are sandwiches and other foods listed in the coming pages that fit the bill for both man and beast. Dogs value good food as much as, or probably even more than, human "foodies" do. After all, they have precious few other distractions in life unless they are "working dogs" or go to work with their person like my Ms. Bea, who held a full-time job as an office greeter and a part-time job as a snack disposal.

Let the Party Go On Forever

With a sedentary life thrust upon dogs who would normally run and jump and explore, it is no big surprise that so many of them are growing as chunky as many of our own species and are developing the same health problems—cancer, heart disease, and stroke—as the hominid population. So, while a party is a time to treat your dog to his favorite foods and try some new ones, too, it is not necessary to abandon healthy eating habits.

The key is to avoid providing too high a dose of rich foods that could add pounds and upset tummies. Even if you bake dog bone cookies that are bigger than your dog's head, as some dog people have been known to do, they can be nutritious and filling without being fattening.

Bear in mind that just as human baby food skips the salt and sugar, these ingredients are widely thought to have no place in good food for dogs either. (I will not say "dog food" as, like many children who know a good thing when they see one, I used to eat my dog's wheat biscuits when I was growing up, so I know that good food crosses species lines!)

What Dogs Like to Eat

My best culinary information came from polling the PETA staff regarding their dogs' desires. The results were surprising. I had always cooked for my dogs and they remained bright-eyed and bushy-tailed into their dotage, but I had no idea I was apparently depriving them of some of the "favorite foods" on this list.

- Pancakes: Apparently many dogs, including Kelly's friend Ellie, Lisa's Sophie, and Mary Beth's beagles, flip out over flapjacks, pine for pancakes, and whine for waffles!
- Peanut butter sandwiches and peanut butter cookies: Well, that works nicely for everyone; serve them to all comers and no one will be drooling over anyone else's plate.
- Banana sandwiches: You can serve all the guests those, or combo them for a PBB. Jennie's Louie takes his heartworm pills "gladly" inside mashed banana. Try banana chips too.

"My beloved Kayla would knock an eighteen-wheeler out of the way for an apple. Once, unbeknownst to us, my coworker Tarina left an apple on top of her computer. While we were out at dinner, seventy-five pound, ten-year-old Kayla clambered to the top of the PC, knocking over an old cup of coffee and reams of papers and making such a mess. We didn't figure out what had happened until the next morning when someone let us know that a 'weird dog' had been 'going berserk' the night before."

—*Daphna Nachminovitch, Director,*
Domestic Animal Abuse Division, PETA

- Frozen peas: Still frozen, right out of the package, these are wolfed down by Robyn's Astrid and at least six other dogs, and cooked peas, sometimes mixed with jasmine rice, go over as a treat.
- Broccoli: This is a huge favorite with a lot of the dogs. Karin Robertson reports that Bodhi "runs through the house, throwing broccoli stalks up in the air before eating them."
- Soy cheese: This stuff is dog catnip!
- Toast with margarine: A certain mixed golden retriever named Stan buries his carefully under a bush in the garden and eats it later when he thinks no one is looking.
- Citrus "spare ribs": Several people reported dogs with a passion for this food made from wheat gluten and available only, as far as we know, from a mail-order Chinese gro-

cer in New York, called May Wah, or online from www.peta mall.com. Click on "food" and then scroll to the bottom to link to VegieWorld.com. Nicole Carter's Henry starts drooling when he smells them cooking, plants himself in the kitchen, and won't be moved.

Oatmeal, popcorn, and pasta also rated highly. And quite a few dogs have a thing for sweet potatoes, baby carrots, honeydew melon, and apple slices. Amy Cooper's angel loves tofu, no matter if it's fried, raw, or in lip-smackingly hot sauce; Roxanne Conwell's dog gets soy yogurt on his birthday and other special occasions.

Doggies Love Doggie Bags!

Watch the leftovers! The dog that production manager Meg Caskey grew up with gave new meaning to the term "doggie bag." She would take any food she could from the table and even went "dumpster diving" for leftovers. This dog, definitely a survivalist, didn't eat the swiped food but stored it away in case of a future famine. She would wait for someone to accidentally leave a dresser drawer open and then hide it in there for safekeeping. Meg says, "It was always nice, pulling out the shirt you planned to wear that day only to find half a buttered bagel sticking to it." If there's a little something left that your dog really likes, pop it into a sandwich bag to surprise her with again in a day or two.

Lindsey Twombly reports that her parent's dog, who shall remain nameless, steals orange slices (why isn't he *given* orange slices?), chews them, and spits the pulp onto the carpet.

Many cities, and not just the big ones like New York, are now lucky enough to boast doggie bakeries, or "barkeries" (check your yellow pages and ask at the local animal shelter in case there is a home baker who caters to dogs). This convenience allows you to shop quickly for your party fare and then use the time you've saved to take your angel on an extra walk. Failing a dog bakery or professional dog baker, you can easily find most of the supplies you need for the following recipes at your local grocery store. Sometimes it means nothing more than simply popping something into the microwave or steaming veggies on your stovetop. So, if you are preparing the food yourself, here are a few suggestions.

Chow Time!

Steamed broccoli and carrots—oh, yes! Odd as it sounds, a lot of dogs go nuts for steamed broccoli and quite a few think steamed carrots are over-the-top delicious. Just steam some whole "trees" of broccoli, stalks and florets, the whole deal, until just barely done, then cool well, but not completely. Some people sprinkle a little nutritional yeast (not brewer's yeast) on them, but I find plain is perfect. It's what the French call *cuisine basse,* food just as Nature intended it. This dish is not only good for dogs, but you can eat the leftovers, if there are any, yourself.

Never, ever keep all the pizza for yourself. Merchandising director Jennie Taylor learned years ago that sharing is a virtue:

"I ordered a pizza," she says, "and, after grabbing a slice, I closed the box lid and set it down on the stove. I was sitting in the living room eating my pizza when in walked Buddy, a black lab mix, with a whole slice of pizza in his mouth. I went to the kitchen to check on the condition of the pizza, and it was still in the box, with the lid closed, on top of the stove. After that we called him 'Little Houdini.'"

> "My sister left two freshly baked cheesecakes on the kitchen counter to cool. He jumped up and knocked both of them down and ate them! He didn't even get sick. My sister was mad and I said, "Hey, let pie-gones be pie-gones."
>
> —*Model Jenny Woods, talking about her dog, Barney*

Now it's time to get cracking—er, cooking. Do try any or all of the recipes that follow, as tastes differ. And when I say "try," I don't mean just make them. Because all the ingredients are good for you, too, *you* can lick the bowl and try the finished product—if your dog leaves anything for you, that is.

All recipes serve a pack of approximately 4 wolfhounds, 10 beagles, or 20 Chihuahuas.

Ralph's Any Occasion Cake

Of course, you can always buy one someone else has made, but this is a dog party favorite.

2 cups whole-wheat flour
2 teaspoons baking powder
⅓ cup vegetable oil
½ cup peanut butter
2 tablespoons water or salt-free veggie broth
2 teaspoons baking powder
⅓ cup vegetable oil or rice milk
2 tablespoons silken tofu
Vegan sour cream or peanut butter (for frosting)

1. Preheat the oven to 350°F.
2. Mix together the flour and baking powder, then add the remaining ingredients, except the sour cream and peanut butter for frosting. Lightly grease a cake pan. Pour the batter into the pan to about the ⅔ full. Bake for 15 to 20 minutes. Let cool and then frost with vegan sour cream or peanut butter.

Bobbie Mullins's Easy Lentil Stew
(Courtesy of Alisa Mullins)

1 pound dry lentils

8 cups vegetable broth

1 bay leaf (remove before serving)

½ teaspoon dried thyme

¼ teaspoon dried sage

2 stalks celery, chopped

2 potatoes, chopped

4 carrots, chopped

A tablespoon of Marmite or Vegemite (available at international supermarkets, in the international aisle of some supermarkets, and in many health food stores)

1. Put the lentils in soup pot. Add the broth and spices and bring to a boil. Reduce the heat and simmer for 1 hour.
2. Add the celery, potatoes, carrots, and Vegemite or Marmite and cook for another 45 minutes to 1 hour. Serve over rice, whole-grain pasta, or oatmeal. Dogs lap it up!

It's a "Dog Eat Dog" World!

Another dog and people favorite: veggie hot dogs like Smart Dogs from Lightlife or Veggie Dogs from Yves. You can serve them "pig in a blanket" style, wrapping one-third of a dog in a salt-free roll (*www.lightlife.com* or *www.yvesveggie.com*).

Let's Have a Dog Party!

Millie's Munchies

(Courtesy of Millie's mom, Brandi Valladolid)

For extra nutrition, add a multivitamin capsule or two and/ or some barley grass juice powder. To make a savory version, add freshly shredded carrots and some Bragg's Liquid Aminos (from the health food store) in place of the molasses and banana.

½ cup peanut butter (preferably all natural)
1 mashed ripe banana
⅓ cup molasses
2 cups whole-wheat flour
½ cup brewer's yeast

1. Mix together the wet ingredients, then add the dry ingredients, mixing with your hands or a mixer. The mixture will be very dense, so add water if needed. Roll into a log, cover with plastic wrap, and chill for about 1 hour.
2. Slice the log into pieces as you would when baking regular cookies, then bake on low heat for 10 minutes or so. If you let the Munchies sit in the oven to cool after you turn the oven off, they will be nice and crunchy.

Carly's Favorite Brownies

(Courtesy of Carly's personal baker, Heather Moore)

6 cups oats (not quick-cooking)

2 cups whole-wheat flour

4 tablespoons soft tofu

⅓ cup corn oil

¾ cup molasses

1 cup rice milk

1 15-ounce can pumpkin

1. Preheat the oven to 325°F.
2. Mix together all the ingredients in a large bowl. Pour the batter into a greased pan. Bake for approximately 1 hour. When cool, cut into squares, and get those chops working!

More Munchies

A multitude of vegan recipes for treats, biscuits, and main dishes you can whip up for your dog can be found at *www.yummyfordogs.org*, including Hummus for Hounds, Cajun Spice Biscuits, and Fido Fudge, along with tips for starting a "Yummy for Dogs" program in your area to help raise money for local animal shelters.

Let's Have a Dog Party!

Bill's Molasses Oat Biscotti

(Courtesy of Bill Killion, in Memory of Carol Killion)

3–4 cups self-rising flour

1 cup rice flour

1 cup cooked oats with ¼ cup margarine

2 cups molasses

¼ cup vegetable oil

Water, as needed

1. Preheat the oven to 320°F.
2. Combine all ingredients, adding the water 1 teaspoon at a time to make the dough. Knead by hand on a floured surface until mixed thoroughly. Form the dough into logs 2 to 2½ inches high. Flatten the logs to make them 6 to 7 inches long by 1½ high. Place on nonstick or lightly oiled baking sheets. Bake for 30 to 40 minutes.
3. Remove and let cool for 10 minutes. Cut into ½- to ¾-inch slices. Place back on baking sheets and bake for an additional 20 minutes or until golden brown. Cool and store in an airtight container or refrigerate.

Ellie's Doggie Biscuits

(courtesy of Ellie's "elder sister," Kelly Fidler)

1 cup cornmeal
3½ cups whole-wheat flour
4 tablespoons instant vegetable stock mix
4 tablespoons artificial bacon bits
¾ cup vegetable oil
1⅓ cup water (approximately)
1 can mushroom gravy (for basting)

1. Preheat the oven to 350°F.
2. Blend together all the ingredients, except the gravy, mixing well. Roll out the mixture to ¼ inch thick on a floured cutting board or other smooth surface. Cut to desired shapes with cookie cutters or a knife. Be creative! For paw-bone- and doghouse-shaped cookie cutters, visit *www .petamall.com.*
3. Bake for approximately 35 to 45 minutes, basting lightly with the gravy. Cool thoroughly before serving.

Ready-Mades

Order your vittles online. Try Pea-Mutt Butter Bites (from Barky Bites Pet Treat Bakery, *www.pet-bandanas.com*; click on "Barky Bites Bakery"), Mr. Barky's (made by PetGuard and available from *www .petacatalog.com* or your local pet supply, grocery, or health food store), peanut butter–flavored "Buddy Biscuits" (baked dog treats available from *www.dogtoys.com*), carob-coated truffles and bone-shaped natural-ingredient flaxseed dog cookies (*www.spotsbakery .ca*), or other goodies from your local dog bakery.

Foods to Avoid When Cooking for or Feeding Dogs

Beware—lots of dogs are allergic to these foods, some of which, like chocolate, can be fatal:

- Avocados (they can cause respiratory distress and stomach inflammation)
- Nuts other than peanuts (they can be toxic to dogs)
- Tomatoes (they cause gastric distress)
- Onions and onion powder (they can damage blood cells and cause anemia in dogs)
- Chocolate (how can life be that cruel?)
- Raisins and grapes (they can cause kidney failure)
- Raw bread dough
- Nutmeg
- Fruit pits and seeds

- Garlic
- Xylitol (a sweetener)
- Cow's milk (can cause digestive upset in any adult animal)

Hors d'Oeuvres for Humans

Dip, it's all about the dip! And you realize that everyone will expect you to serve it in dog bowls, don't you? If you are lucky, you might even find individual ones with the guests' names already printed on them, or you can go to one of the "paint it yourself" stores and decorate ceramic paw print bowls. Stainless steel ones are easy to clean and nothing sticks to them. And plastic isn't so bad either. But I'd opt for the ceramic so as to keep the taste of the food true and fresh.

Some of the recipes that follow came from celebrities who not only look after their figures, but their dogs as well. They appear, with many others, in the *PETA Celebrity Cookbook*.

Ooh, Look! A Squirrel: Something to Distract Dogs While You Eat

Dogs should always eat first, of course, as it is hideously rude to keep any guest waiting. But dogs usually also want to eat second and last, as well. If you need to distract your dog during human feeding time, you might try the Twist 'n Treat, a toy that unscrews for easy loading of treats but takes a bit of doing for your dog to open it. That way, it takes more time and some exercise for your dog to get at the food in front of him and the food on your plate. The Twist 'n Treat is available from *www.tail-waggers.com*.

Alicia Silverstone's Steamy, Creamy Artichoke Dip

Alicia Silverstone loves her Rottweiler/pit bull/Doberman mix, a rescued street dog named Samson, and is always doing charitable deeds by pounding the pavement looking for homes for dogs who have no place to hang their hats. Alicia is also the absolute picture of health and vitality, and so who better to borrow a recipe from? Here is Alicia's favorite party dip.

> 2 (8-ounce) cans quartered artichoke hearts
> 1 cup vegan mayonnaise
> 1 cup soy Parmesan "cheese"
> 1 teaspoon paprika
> Garlic powder to taste

1. Preheat the oven to 350°F.
2. Drain the liquid from the artichokes; mash and combine with the other ingredients. Scoop into a casserole dish and bake for 30 minutes. Sprinkle additional paprika on top before serving. Serve with chips, toasted and cut pita bread, or sliced fresh veggies.

Makes 10 servings

William Shatner's Layered Dip
Mexicana de Frijoles

Mr. Shatner says of this dip, "Other than our swimming pool, this is the best dip around!"

- 2 (12-ounce) cans vegetarian refried beans
- ⅔ cup vegan mayonnaise
- 1 cup vegan sour cream
- 1 packet taco seasoning
- 2 (4-ounce) cans chopped green chilies, drained
- 2 large ripe avocados, peeled and pitted
- 2 teaspoons lime juice
- 1 teaspoon garlic powder, or 4 teaspoons fresh-minced garlic
- 1 cup chopped green onions
- 2 cups diced tomatoes
- 2 (4-ounce) cans sliced black olives

Spread refried beans evenly on a large serving platter. In a bowl, combine the mayonnaise, sour cream, and taco seasoning. Spread evenly over the beans. Spoon the green chilies as evenly as possible over the taco seasoning mixture. In a separate bowl, combine the avocados, lime juice, and garlic. Mix well and spread evenly over the chilies. Finally, top with the green onions, tomatoes, and black olives.

Makes 9–12 servings

Grant Aleksander and Sherry Ramsey's Great Guacamole

Grant and Sherry consider their dogs to be in the category of All My Children *and say their dogs have been a* Guiding Light *in their work to help homeless dogs. If that doesn't give you a clue. . . .*

1 ripe tomato

2 tablespoons finely minced white onion

3 jalapeño chilies, finely chopped
   Sea salt, to taste

3 large avocados

2 tablespoons finely minced fresh cilantro
   Extra tomato for garnish

Combine the tomato, onion, chilies, and salt in a small bowl or a *molcajete* (mortar and pestle). Mash with a pestle or spoon into a coarse paste. Halve the avocados, remove the pits, and scoop the flesh into the mix. Add the cilantro and mix again. Add more salt to taste if desired, and garnish with tomatoes. Serve at once.

Makes 10 servings

Jackie Chan's Corn Chowder

Jackie Chan is not only a dog's best friend and big defender, but he cares for all animals.

> 5 medium potatoes, peeled and chopped
> 3 cups water or vegetable broth
> 2 teaspoons vegetable oil or water
> 1 medium onion, finely chopped
> 2 stalks celery, diced
>   Salt and pepper, to taste
> 1 cup plain soy milk
> 2½ cups corn kernels

1. In a medium saucepan, boil the potatoes in the water or broth for 20 minutes. While the potatoes are cooking, heat the oil or water in a medium frying pan over medium heat. Add the onion, celery, salt, and pepper. Cook until just tender, about 5 to 7 minutes.
2. When the potatoes are soft, remove them from the pan and reserve the stock. Blend the potatoes with the soy milk in a blender or food processor until smooth. Return the soup to the saucepan and stir in the corn, onion mixture, and enough of the reserved stock to achieve a creamy, thick consistency. Heat thoroughly before serving.

Makes 6 servings

Moby's Zucchini Sticks with Horseradish Dip

- 1 cup unbleached all-purpose flour
  Salt and pepper, to taste
- 2 teaspoons garlic powder
- 4 medium zucchini, cut in half and sliced lengthwise
- 2 tablespoons olive oil

For the dip:
- 1 cup Eggless Mayonnaise (see recipe that follows)
- 3-4 tablespoons prepared horseradish
  Salt, to taste

1. Combine the flour, salt, pepper, and garlic powder. Dip the zucchini sticks into the flour mixture and coat well.
2. In a large skillet, heat the olive oil over medium heat. Sauté the zucchini for about 5 minutes, then place it on a paper towel to soak up any excess oil.
3. For the dip, combine the mayonnaise, horseradish, and salt. Arrange the zucchini sticks on a platter. Pour the horseradish dip into a small bowl and serve with the zucchini.

Makes 6 to 8 servings

Eggless Mayonnaise

3 tablespoons lemon juice

½ cup soy milk, unflavored

¼ teaspoon salt

¼ teaspoon paprika

¼ teaspoon prepared mustard

6 tablespoons vegetable oil

1. Put all the ingredients except the oil into a blender. Blend on the lowest speed. Gradually—one drop at a time, really!—add the oil until the mixture starts to thicken. Continue blending until thickened and smooth.
2. Transfer to a jar and store in the refrigerator.

What's for Dessert?

If your sweet tooth is calling, try these dairy-free delights: Rice Dream and Soy Dream Non-dairy Frozen Desserts (*www.tastethe dream.com*), So Delicious Dairy-free Desserts (*www.turtlemountain .com*), and Tofutti and Tofutti Cuties (*www.tofutti.com*). Or, if you'd like to make your own, read Jeff Rogers' *Vice Cream: Over 70 Sinfully Delicious Dairy-Free Delights.* For a tasty treat that your dog will enjoy, try Frosty Paws, a soy-based "ice cream" treat. It's available in some pet supply stores, or visit *www.frostypawstreats .com* and order a party pack!

Hair of the Dog: For the Party or to Curl Up with Later

Drinking and driving don't mix, but dogs and grogs can go nicely. If you plan to serve cocktails at your party, browse the short selection of appropriately themed recipes—or create your own concoction. Name it after the guest of honor, perhaps a Millie's Manhattan or a Jolly Rover complete with a dog lollipop. For more cocktail recipe ideas, visit *www.globalgourmet.com*.

Iced Chamomile Cranberry Cocktail

2 cups brewed chamomile tea
½ cup cranberry juice cocktail (unsweetened or not)
Sugar, to taste

Steep the tea for 6 to 8 minutes, to desired strength. Mix with the juice. Stir in the sugar. Pour over ice. Place a mint sprig on top. This should put you softly to sleep.

Dog's Nose

1½ ounces gin
1 bottle beer (lager, ale, porter, or stout)
Nutmeg (optional)

Pour the gin into a tall glass. Fill with the beer. Dust with nutmeg if you use porter. Serve.

Barking Dog

1 ounce gin
¾ ounce dry vermouth
¾ ounce sweet vermouth
2 dashes Calisay (a Spanish quinine-based herbal digestive liqueur that's rather good if you have overeaten or are in danger of getting leg cramps)

Mix together all the ingredients. Serve in a cocktail glass with a cherry on top.

Salty Dog

2 ounces vodka (Grey Goose for those of you with field dogs; a Russian brand if you have a borzoi or Russian wolfhound, perhaps)
5 ounces grapefruit juice
2 teaspoons salt
1 lime wedge

Mix together all the ingredients in a shaker and shake like a dog coming out of the river.

As for wines, luckily lots of vintners and vineyard owners love dogs! Some of the very first people to plant grapes on a hillside in North America named their first wines after their dogs. If you start looking for a wine that will suit your party theme, there's almost no limit to what you will find, from Virginia Chateau Morrisette's Blushing Dog and Black Dog to Dunham Cellars' Three Legged Red (named after Port, a puppy who lost a leg to a pit bull attack), California's Mutt Lynch Winery's Canis Major Syrah, Chardonnay Unleashed, and my favorite, Merlot Over and Play Dead (all named in honor of the founder's dog, Brenda, whose picture is featured on the vineyard's Web site).

Graeser Winery celebrated its new four-legged friend Black Jack by announcing, "We know dogs come in packs, and so we have put together a great three-pack. One bottle each of the 2002 Simba's Sinful Zin, 2002 Alex Ruff Red, and 2002 Two Dog Merlot." And Gallo's high-end, Provence-inspired French wine "Red Bicyclette" is delicious. This wine label features a cartoon of a little dog running happily behind a two-wheeler, baguette clamped firmly in his mouth.

Finally, although there are almost as many dogs in the alcohol business as there are grapes, this being a rich topic, Hawthorne Mountain Vineyards' "See Ya Later" ranch series wines feature the founder and grape grower Major Hugh Fraser's old Border collie (now long gone, as is Major Fraser) on the label, his dog appearing in cartoon form, rendered in white and wearing little angel wings!

To celebrate its dog friends and their human companions, the wine country of California holds several "dog day afternoons" every summer. Stryker Sonoma Winery puts the price of admission toward a dog charity, like Paws for a Cause, and the dogs can participate in romps and obedience classes, and can even paint if they like! Small dogs can be carried into the tasting rooms so that their guardians can imbibe, and all dogs are welcomed with biscuits and other refreshments.

Winery Web Sites

Chateau Morrissette: *www.chateaumorrissette.com*
Dunham Cellars: *www.dunhamcellars.com*
Mutt Lynch Winery: *www.muttlynchwinery.com*
Hawthorne Mountain Vineyards: *www.hmvineyard.com*
Graeser Winery: *www.graeserwinery.com*
Gallo's Red Bicyclette: *www.redbicyclette.com*

Put Your Dog on the Label

It's also easy to get your own labels for wine bottles. You can send a photograph or sketch of the guest of honor or the whole family or whatever you think sets the tone, and have them made up into labels to commemorate the party. Wine companies like Hair-o'-the-Dog will help you with that (*www.hair-o-the-dog.com*), or check with your local wineries if they offer the service.

There really is something for everyone and to ensure that every dog can have his day. For example, if you or your dog is a truck enthusiast, *www.cafepress.com* offers already-designed "Dogs on Trucks" labels for $3 each. You will have to make or buy the wine. Just remember not to drink and drive!

11
a BEDTIME STORY
with a Happy Ending

"He taught me the joy of a much longer sunrise walk to see the new day."

—*Thomas D. Murray,*
talking about his dog, George

One of the most moving stories I have ever come across about the relationship between a caring soul and a dog is an editorial entitled "What George Taught Us," by Thomas D. Murray. I can't resist sharing it with you here. Read it to yourself or out loud to dogs and other small family members.

When Mr. Murray, a writer, lost his dog to old age, he began to think back on what joy his dog had brought into his life and what he had not noticed about his dog while George was alive. I have kept a copy of that article in my files. I know the truth of it, for when my dogs died, I began to wish I had been more patient and considerate.

When the Murray family got George, they had to teach him to go up and down stairs as he'd lived his life on one floor.

Murray wrote: "I think that's the only thing we ever taught him in thirteen years, and it was mostly desperation that made me finally give up and conclude that maybe this dog didn't come to us to learn, but to teach, though it took me a while to understand the lessons."

Murray says he started out trying to teach George by using a rolled-up newspaper to stop his barking and dancing through the house every time the doorbell rang or he heard a car in the driveway. "I think he was trying to make me understand," concludes Murray, "that a friend at the door, even a stranger or the mailman, can be a nice little diversion on a humdrum day, and something to celebrate with a little excitement."

Murray says George was impatient whenever his food was being fixed, "prancing around the kitchen, standing on his rear legs and then gulping down a full bowl almost before it was set in front of him on the floor." No matter what was said or done to calm him down, George never stopped this excitement, probably, as Murray decided, "to remind me of the pure joy of wanting and waiting for something, and, by always wagging his tail the entire time he was eating, demonstrating that gratefulness is a priceless part of good manners and doesn't cost a thing."

Early on, Murray had tried to get George to hurry up and finish his business in the yard and come back inside. "In time," he says, "he taught me the joy of a much longer sunrise walk to see the new day, even in winter, and another after dinner to help put the day's work and worries in perspective. I think I grew to look forward to those walks as much as George did."

There are many more lessons George taught the family over time, but my favorite is about Christmas celebrations. The Murrays thought that they would make Christmastime special by putting a red bow on George's collar and giving him some extra treats but realized that on all the days that weren't Christmas, George was trying to show them that it was possible to spread that feeling of anticipation and happiness over the whole year, not just when the holly decorations and the tree were put up. In other words, George's lesson was "that the only presents that meant much of anything to him were those that were waiting for him, not just on Christmas, but every morning of the year—his family, his friends, his freedom, and not too many baths."

12 *Time to Put Up* YOUR FEET

"She can't stand to fall asleep while anyone else is awake, so she sits up with her eyes shut and her head occasionally falling to one side."

—Animal rights activist Sarah McCluskey,
talking about her dog, Nola

Your party has been a success and now it's time for you to soak your feet, pour yourself a cocktail, virgin or not (the cocktail, I mean—I'm not getting personal), and relax.

You and your dog will benefit from total quiet after the melee or, if you must, a little classical music. Research studies show that the "Mozart Effect" (*www.mozarteffects.com*) not only calms children and chickens but also soothes even the savage beast's breast as well. A study conducted by Queen's Hospital and the National Canine Defence League in a shelter for lost and unwanted dogs in Belfast, Northern Ireland, showed that dogs relaxed and barked less frequently when listening to Mozart.

Spoiled for choice? Let someone else not only wash the dishes but also select the music by putting on the aptly named *The Most Relaxing Classical Album in the World . . . Ever*! This "album" has choice pieces by Tchaikovsky, Bach, Beethoven, Debussy's dreamy "Clair de Lune," and the great man of the Effect himself, Herr Wolfgang Amadeus Mozart (available on *www.amazon.com*).

Play all music softly when dogs are present. In addition to wildly sensitive noses, they have such acutely sensitive hearing that they can hear a cricket cleaning her antennae. Such talent is evidenced by your dog's prompt, almost magical, appearance from the far upstairs bedroom when a refrigerator door is quietly opened in the kitchen. They hear things you and I don't. If this means anything to you, our highest range is 20kHz and theirs is 45kHz. That means they hear a much greater range of sounds. It also means there's nothing much you can get away with. Most importantly, it makes raising your voice to a dog, who apparently *already* thinks you are yelling, an *extremely* mean thing to do.

One thing about high-frequency sounds: As beautiful and moving as are Yehudi Menuhin's works, dogs trying to sleep can find the violin as disturbing as most of us who weren't born in Scotland find the bagpipes. And after all, regardless of breed, what you want at this point is well expressed in E. V. Lucas's poem, "The Pekingese":

"The Pekingese
Adore their ease
And slumber like the dead;
In comfort curled
They view the world
As one unending bed."

If you have done your job well, your dog will be off to bed to dream of the happiest day in her life.

13 *Make* EVERY DAY a *Party*

"When he is irritated with us—let's say we're talking on the phone or petting Ginger—he goes into the closet and pouts, sitting behind all the clothes with just his tail sticking out."

—Campaign manager Megan Hartman, talking about her dog, Cinnamon

Does your dog think life with you is like having a party every day? Have you ever wondered "How good am I from my dog's point of view?" When you see your dog lying flat out on the floor, eyes tightly shut, legs moving slightly, is he dreaming of chasing rabbits through a meadow? No. He is dreaming of the perfect you. Those twitching whiskers are memories of your foibles. Your dog has firm ideas about what he wants in a lifetime companion, although, unlike picky cats, he'll settle for pretty much any old thing. But will you let him settle for so little?

Ask yourself, are you your dog's Prince Charming or Cinderella? Or are you a bit of a twit when it comes to realizing what he or she needs?

No one likes self-evaluations, do they? But we must be brave. After all, your dog is probably far too polite to point out your shortcomings. Or perhaps he does give you hints by sulking in the corner once in a while or giving you a long sideways glance that is the canine equivalent of an archly raised eyebrow. Now is the time to give him or her the greatest gift next to a leashless existence and a self-opening refrigerator: a reformed you. Take this little quiz and see how you rate.

Give yourself one point for every statement that applies:

1. I have spayed/neutered my dog (no excuse if your dog is young; sterilization surgery can now be performed when your dog is only twelve weeks old).
2. I never let my dog out unattended unless in a fully enclosed, secure area.

3. I give him fresh water in his bowl and I clean it carefully and rinse it every day.
4. I am always on time with meals.
5. I don't smoke in the vicinity of my dog's sensitive nose and lungs. (A Colorado State University study, one of many, concluded that dogs are at a 60 percent greater risk of lung cancer in smoking households. This higher incidence was specifically found among long-nosed breed dogs such as collies.)
6. I keep his veterinarian's number in my wallet and by the phones.
7. My dog gets at least three good walks, including a really long one, every day, even on days when I'm so late for work I may be fired (not a bad thing, as it would give you more time to enjoy with your dog).
8. I take time to play with my dog every single day, no matter what, even on days when I feel bilious or have an important date (who might like to play with you and your dog instead of going out somewhere fancy).
9. I never forget to kiss my dog goodbye when I leave home (give yourself two points if you never leave home except to walk your dog).
10. I always bring home a present (this can be as small and inexpensive as a dried leaf or stick; the important thing is to make an Academy Award–style fuss over the presentation).

11. I have provided for my dog in the event of my death (you can take steps by naming a caretaker for him or her in your will, setting aside money in a trust fund, or making a direct bequest to a trusted caregiver or trusted animal charity).

12. There is a sticker on my front and back doors that reads, "In the event of an emergency, please rescue my [state number] dogs."

13. This would be a very unlucky number indeed for my dog if he had been let out of my yard by a careless meter reader or other visitor and I hadn't equipped him with a tag with my current address and phone numbers, including my cell phone number, on it. Fortunately, I have.

14. I would never be so miserable as to dock my dog's beautiful tail or crop her ears (you may excuse yourself if someone else did this before you discovered that dogs look splendid with flags instead of stumps and floppy ears instead of masts).

15. I always take my dog with me when I go on vacation.

16. I never board my dog away from home when I travel (give yourself two points if you never travel).

17. I have learned to groom my dog myself or I patronize a groomer who allows me to watch my dog being groomed rather than whisking him out of sight to be bathed or clipped.

18. I never allow my dog to be kept overnight at the veterinarian (you may still get a point if the only exception is in the case of extremely serious injury or illness and where the

vet's office is one of those emergency ones that is open and attended all night. But there is no sense in abandoning an already distressed dog to a smelly, strange, usually uncomfortable cage, surrounded by wailing animals and the pungent smell of disinfectant and other patients' feces when, with some effort, you can look after your dog in your own bedroom and call a vet if there's a problem).

19. I will never fly my dog in the cargo hold of a plane.
20. I will never make a lot of noise when my dog is trying to sleep.
21. I will not brush my teeth or put the coffee on before I've walked my dog in the morning.
22. I will never swat at, swear at, or otherwise debase my dog.
23. I will never fail to answer politely if my dog says something to me and to thank my dog for alerting me to people coming to the door.
24. I will never oust my dog from any furniture.
25. I will never give away my dog to anyone else (the only excuses are imprisonment, hospitalization, incapacity, and military dispatch in times of war, although you can probably take your dog to Canada with you).
26. I would never leave children, strangers, or people whose reliability I have not verified in charge of my dog.
27. I have micro-chipped my dog for safety's sake.
28. I feed my dog before I feed myself.
29. I do not leave my dog in a crate but have hired a dog walker or installed a dog door.

30. I believe my dog is a blessing, a privilege to know, and that I am lucky to have his or her friendship.

How did you score?

Only your dog is perfect, but any score below twenty points on this basic care quiz demands your immediate remedial training. Remember every time you have resolved to eat less fat and then ordered the fries? This is not like that. This is serious business. You must decide immediately to change your stripes. I'm surprised that you can live with yourself. Throwing a dog party is a must; your dog needs a break. But a whole lot of remedial work is also in the cards.

If you scored twenty to twenty-five points you simply have to shape up. Where are you failing? What can you do right away to overcome the problem? Put a note on your dashboard? Change a plan? Go shopping for your dog? Throw a dog party? Some extra effort is definitely required here.

Twenty-eight points or higher? I'll be moving in with you shortly.

14

Sponsor a "Party" for a NEGLECTED DOG

"Therefore is a man called holy."

—*Dhammapada, Buddhist Scripture*

I mentioned in the dedication to this book that there are many wonderful dogs who never get so much as a pat on the head or a kind word, let alone a party. Karen Porreca, PETA's librarian, makes a donation in the name, and in honor, of each of her dogs on their birthdays. She has made a big difference. Somewhere in North Carolina, where there is not even a law that requires shelter in winter for a dog, there are dogs with chew toys and bedding, thanks to the love Shandy, Darby, Rogan, Koro, and Druzhok have shared with Karen.

Perhaps you would be interested in bringing a little joy to one of these underprivileged dogs? To them, a "party" means something extremely basic. It might just mean that someone cares and stops to check on them and brings them some practical help, perhaps even a toy.

There is a hidden world out there that few of those of us who read this book will ever see. Part of it is deep in the countryside where poor people still live in what were once shacks, in beaten-up trailers in fields, in low-income neighborhoods where everyone is worried that what little they have might be stolen and has a dog on guard to protect it. If these dogs could speak, perhaps they would recite the "Chained Dog's Plea" written by Edith Lassen Johnson ©PETA:

"I wish someone would tell me
What it is that I've done wrong
Why do I have to stay chained up
And left alone so long? . . .

All I had, you see, was love.
I wish they would explain
Why they said they wanted mine,
And then left it on a chain."

PETA's Community Animal Project (CAP) goes into those areas to find these cheap burglar alarms, the forgotten dogs, and bring them some relief from a hard life that usually does not end well. The dogs they find (and you can see their photographs on *www.helpinganimals.com*) are kept permanently chained like bicycles. There are many thousands, if not millions, of them in cities, towns, and in the country.

These lonely, neglected dogs will never experience the joy of a party, but, thanks to the workers and volunteers of organizations like CAP, who drive out, vigilantly searching and listening for them, some of them will get what, to them, is the equivalent: a sturdy doghouse that doesn't leak and has a real floor, a flexible tie-out to replace the heavy chain staked into the ground to hold them prisoner, some warm straw to curl up in when the temperatures drop, a bucket that doesn't tip over in the summer leaving them parched, and . . . a chewy, something they likely have never seen before.

If you would like to sponsor a "dog party" for one of these dogs, you will make them very happy indeed. When I called hip-hop mogul Russell Simmons and told him what we were seeing out there in the dead of winter, he immediately recorded a radio spot, asking people to "respect your dogs as you would yourself." And when I showed photographs of the dogs' living conditions to Kimora Lee Simmons, the model and founder of Baby Phat, who stops on the street if she sees a dog being abused, she became so upset that she sponsored help for 100 dogs, just like that! Two good deeds. Perhaps two drops in the bucket, but wonderful drops that the dogs need to feel many more of.

Robert Louis Stevenson wrote:

"You think those dogs will not be in Heaven!

I tell you they will be there long before any of us."

Considering the hell on earth the ones I'm referring to go through, we might wish to give them a little bit of what to them is surely heaven, long before their time is up!

Some Ways to Help

Make your donation to PETA (and mark it for use by Community Animal Project) c/o PETA, 501 Front St., Norfolk, VA 23510, or go to *www .helpinganimals.com* for more information on dog sponsorship.

Enquire locally about programs that bring doghouses, sterilization, medical care, and toys to neglected dogs. See the Resources section for other organizations that can hook you up to help.

Children can also help. For example, students at Badshot Lea Village Infant School in Farnham, Surrey, England, held a "Toys for Dogs" Day. Each child made or brought a toy to be sold. The children raised almost $200 to help hearing ear dogs.

CONCLUSION
The Tail End

"I am thankful for the mess to clean up after a party because it means I have been surrounded by friends."

—*Poet Nancy J. Carmody*

The comedian Steven Wright once said, "A conclusion is the place where you got tired of thinking." Hopefully it's your dog who is tired. If you have done a good job, he may be sinking off into dreamland to conjure up visions of his happiest moments with the one he loves: you, the giver of all things.

One party may be over, but there are lots more ahead. You have an awe-inspiring task on your hands, the responsibility and duty to provide love and lasting entertainment to this dear soul who gives you so much.

I hope this book has been useful. Please let me know about your dog, your dog's personality, quirks, and adventures, and the parties you've had. You can reach me at PETA, 501 Front St., Norfolk, VA 23510, or *www.peta.org*.

Here's to you and your dog's happiness.

Can't Wait to See You at My Dog Party!

When: _____

Where: _____

What: Barking, treats, liquid refreshments, games

Bring: Yourself, your lovely dog _____, and, if you like, a toy for everyone to play with

Dress: Casual, we'll provide the paw prints!

RSVP to 555-5555

Love,

_____

(your dog's name)

THIS COUPON ENTITLES
MY WONDERFUL DOG

_____

to a **one-hour walk**
with me!

THIS COUPON ENTITLES
MY WONDERFUL DOG

_____

to a **trip to the beach**
with me!

THIS COUPON ENTITLES
MY WONDERFUL DOG

_____

to a **half day at the park**
with me and all his/her
doggie friends!

THIS COUPON ENTITLES
MY WONDERFUL DOG

_____

to a **half-day hike** with
me at our favorite
hiking spot!

THIS COUPON ENTITLES
MY WONDERFUL DOG

_____

to a **trip to the pet
supply store** to choose
his/her own toy!

THIS COUPON ENTITLES
MY WONDERFUL DOG

_____

to a **drive-and-sniff**
with me! (I'll drive!)

THIS COUPON ENTITLES
MY WONDERFUL DOG

_____

to a **game of Frisbee**
with me!

THIS COUPON ENTITLES
MY WONDERFUL DOG

_____

to a **howl-a-thon**
with me!

THIS COUPON ENTITLES
MY WONDERFUL DOG

_____

to a **batch of home-
baked doggie treats!**

RESOURCES

Books

Adler, Judith, and Toni Tucker. *Zen Dog* (New York: Clarkson Potter, 2001).

Anderson, Allen and Linda. *Angel Dogs: Divine Messengers of Love* (Novato, CA: New World Library, 2005).

Arden, Andrea. *Dog-Friendly Dog Training* (New York: Hungry Minds, 2000).

Ballner, Maryjean. *Dog Massage: A Whiskers-to-Tail Guide to Your Dog's Ultimate Petting Experience* (New York: St. Martin's Press, 2000).

Banks, Joan. *Petfinder.com Presents: Second Chances: Inspiring Stories of Dog Adoption* (Avon, MA: Adams Media, 2006).

Brilliant, Jennifer, and William Berloni. *Doga: Yoga for Dogs* (San Francisco: Chronicle Books, 2003).

Brown, Doug, and Kaori A. Brown. *Bad Dog Chronicles: True Tales of Trouble Only a Best Friend Can Get Away With* (New York: Howell Book House, 2000). Available from *www.baddogs.com.*

Buckle, Jane. *How to Massage Your Dog* (New York: Howell Book House, 1995).

Cole, Joanna, and Stephanie Calmenson. *Give a Dog a Bone: Stories, Poems, Jokes and Riddles About Dogs* (Jefferson City, MO: Scholastic, 1999).

Editors of *The Bark* Magazine. *Dog Is My Co-Pilot: Great Writers on the World's Oldest Friendship* (New York: Crown, 2003).

Fisher, Betty, and Suzanne Delzio. *Caninestein: Unleashing the Genius in Your Dog* (New York: HarperCollins, 1997).

Fox, Michael W. *The Healing Touch for Dogs: The Proven Massage Program for Dogs,* Revised Edition (New York: Newmarket Press, 2004).

Franklin, R. M. *Captain Loxley's Little Dog and Lassie the Life-Saving Collie: Hero Dogs of the First World War Associated with the Sinking of the H.M.S. Formidable.* (West Sussex, UK: Diggory Press, 2005).

Hunter, Roy. *Fun Nosework* (Franklin, NY: Howln Moon Press, 1996).

Kipling, Rudyard. *Thy Servant, a Dog and Other Stories: Rudyard Kipling Centenary Editions* (London: Pan Macmillan, 1982).

Knapp, Caroline. *Pack of Two* (New York: Dial Press, 1998).

Lofting, Hugh. *The Voyages of Dr. Doolittle* (New York: Signet Classics, 2000).

Quasha, Jennifer. *The Dog Lover's Book of Crafts: 50 Home Decorations that Celebrate Man's Best Friend* (New York: St. Martin's/ Griffin, 2001).

Tellington-Jones, Linda. *Getting in Touch with Your Dog: A Gentle Approach to Influencing Behavior, Health, and Performance* (North Pomfret, VT: Trafalgar Square Publishing, 2001).

Tellington-Jones, Linda. *The Tellington TTouch: A Revolutionary Natural Method to Train and Care for Your Favorite Animal* (New York: Penguin Putnam, 1993).

Various contributors. *The Dog's Guide to Surfing: Hanging Ten with Man's Best Friend* (San Francisco: TBC-Cafe Publishing). This collection of stories and photos can be purchased at *www.lastgasp.com.*

Whalen-Shaw, Patricia. *Canine Massage* (Mansfield, OH: Bookmasters, 2000).

Magazines

The Bark, "an alternative magazine for modern dog enthusiasts" at *www.thebark.com.*

The Hollywood Dog, at *www.hollywooddog.com.*

The New York Dog, at *www.thenewyorkdog.com.*

Organizations that Help Neglected Dogs

Alley Animals
www.alleyanimals.org
This small rescue group helps needy dogs (and cats) in the Baltimore area.

Coalition for the DC Animal Shelter
http://hometown.aol.com/dcshelter
This all-volunteer group works to ensure that Washington, DC's animal control and shelter programs are fully funded and run by a qualified organization.

GREY2K USA

www.grey2kusa.org

This group works tirelessly to educate the public about the cruelty of greyhound racing, to protect greyhounds through legislation and other means, and ultimately to end this horrific industry.

Johnston County Animal Protection

http://jcapl.org/index.htm

The mission statement of the Johnston County Animal Protection League is to promote animal welfare through advocacy, protection, humane education, and reduction of pet overpopulation.

Kuranda beds, Donate-a-Bed program

www.kuranda.com/shop/donate.asp

This maker of unique, comfy dog beds has a special program that enables you to donate a dog bed to the shelter of your choice at a discounted price.

PETA

501 Front St.
Norfolk, VA 23510
www.helpinganimals.com and *www.peta.org*

PETA's many programs to help dogs include SNIP (Spay/Neuter Immediately, Please!), a mobile spay/neuter clinic that travels to low-income neighborhoods in Virginia and North Carolina offering free or low-cost sterilization surgeries. SNIP workers perform an average of twenty-five surgeries a day, preventing the births of thousands of unwanted animals.

Planned Pethood Clinic

plannedpethoodrockymount @yahoo.com

The Planned Pethood Low Cost Spay Neuter Clinic has performed well over 20,000 spay/neuter surgeries since opening their doors in July 2000.

SOI Dog Foundation

www.soidog.org

This group works to make life better for the hundreds of homeless dogs living in Phuket, Thailand ("soi" means "street"), providing vet care, spay/neuter services, and working with the local government and community to help solve the overpopulation problem.